THE
INCEPTION
OF THE
CHURCH
BEFORE
CREATION
WITH
CHRIST
AS THE
HEAD
OF THE
CHURCH
IN HIS
THREE OFFICES

Dr. Sabelo Sam Gasela Mhlanga

WESTBOW
PRESS®
A DIVISION OF THOMAS NELSON
& ZONDERVAN

WestBow Press books may be ordered through booksellers or by contacting:

WestBow Press
A Division of Thomas Nelson & Zondervan
1663 Liberty Drive
Bloomington, IN 47403
www.westbowpress.com
844-714-3454

Scripture taken from the King James Version of the Bible.

ISBN: 978-1-6642-1425-5 (sc)
ISBN: 978-1-6642-1426-2 (e)

Print information available on the last page.

WestBow Press rev. date: 12/09/2020

CONTENTS

Acknowledgements vii
Abstract ix

Chapter 1: Introduction.. 1
The inception of the Church.. 1
The Three-Fold Office of Christ 2
The Lessons for the Church Today: Universal and Africa 3
Organization 4
Background.. 5

Chapter 2: The Church's Inception Historically................................... 7
Old Testament 7
New Testament.. 16
Patristic Period: Augustine 20
Medieval Period: Thomas Aquinas.. 26
Reformation Period: John Calvin.. 29
Post-Reformation Period: John Bunyan 31
Evangelical Period: George Whitefield 33
Conclusion 35

Chapter 3: The Church's Inception Biblically 36
The Church's inception Before Creation... 36
The Church's inception from the Triune-Godhead 37
Election.. 42
Predestination 48
Redemption and Adoption... 52
Visible and Invisible Church.. 56

Conclusion 63

Chapter 4: The Church's Inception Theologically 64
The Threefold Office of Christ 64
Christ as Prophet 65
Christ as Priest 68
Christ as King 72
Conclusion 74

Chapter 5: The Church's Inception Practically 75
The Universal Church 76
The African Church 82
Conclusion 90

Chapter 6: The Church's Inception Summarized 92

Bibliography 95

ACKNOWLEDGEMENTS

The thesis is dedicated to my mother, Josephine, and my late father, Joseph Gasela Mhlanga, who impacted my life positively to regard all human beings as equal and that all human beings are created in the image of God. My appreciation goes to my lovely wife, Judith, for her prayers, patience, advice, and encouragement whenever we make decisions for the family. I thank my lovely and always cheerful children and our five children, Blessing-Qhawe, Shalom-Sinqobile, Prosper-Thando, Emmanuel-Nkosi and Joseph Sam-Nkosana for their prayers and playing with me even if I am tired.

Above all, I thank my Lord and Savior Jesus Christ and God the Father for His protection, provision and guidance through the Holy Spirit. All the glory, majesty, and honor be to God the Almighty.

The author is indebted to the following people for their remarkable contribution, inspiration, and encouragements. I thank my supervisor, Dr. Joel Beeke, for his academic and theological expertise in guiding me through this thesis. He is an experienced and renowned author. Henk Kleyn has been an encouragement to me all the way through and for giving me valuable and good advice. I would like to extend my profound gratitude to all the members of my extended family, the Gasela-Mhlanga family and friends such as Koos and Elsa, Antoine and Nicholine, Taebok and his wife, Brain Kamwendo, Brian Najapfoor and Calvin Beeke for all their moral and spiritual support.

ABSTRACT

This thesis advocates that the church's inception was before creation. It contends that the Reformers' contributions to ecclesiology are valuable for presenting an accurate portrayal of the biblical model of the church. This book will also examine and suggest the answer to the question that the church's inception was before creation and goes on into the eternal future with Christ as the Head of the church.

The church did not begin in the Old Testament or in the New Testament but began in eternity past. Christ is eternal and as the Head (husband) of the church (wife), she is also eternal in His mind. Given the fact that Christ is eternal, the conclusion is that He cannot be the head of a merely temporary body, (the church). The incarnation was God's means to redeem His bride so that He would be with her for eternity. As God the Son, He has been the Head of the church before the creation, and the incarnation was a means by which He would gain her redemption, and now He continues to be her head for the eternal. The three-fold office of Christ (prophet, priest, king) was and is a pure manifestations of Christ to humanity to show that He loves the church (the elect) and is in the process of saving and sanctifying her.

Some scholars believe that the church's inception was in the Old Testament and other scholars suggest that the church began in the New Testament. The church in Africa is in danger of being defiled by syncretism and acculturation. This thesis will show how the church in Africa ought to face these challenges by looking to Jesus, her formula from eternity past, her Builder in time and her Lord to all eternity. In this thesis I show why it is important for today's universal church-also in my native continent of Africa-to maintain the church was conceived in God's mind from eternity past.

■ CHAPTER 1 ■

INTRODUCTION

THE INCEPTION OF THE CHURCH

This thesis seeks to address, validate, examine and to suggest an answer to the question that the church's inception was before creation and goes on into eternity. Many scholars have argued that the church began in the Old Testament at Mount Sinai while others argued that the church began in the New Testament at Pentecost. The argument for this paper is that the church's inception was from eternity past and goes on into all eternity. If Christ is the Head of the church and if He is eternal, then it follows that the church will go on eternally and the members of the body of Christ will live eternally with the bridegroom, Christ Jesus. It is true that the church's manifestation started in the Old Testament and continued in the New Testament with the incarnation: the birth, death, and resurrection of Christ. But the plan and inception of the church was rooted in the Trinity, the Godhead. Christ in His three-fold office came to save His fallen bride. It is therefore imperative not to separate Christ with his three-fold office from the church because the church cannot exist without Christ.

Ivor Davidson says, "Jesus regarded the temple in Jerusalem as the supreme site of God's holy presence on earth, the place where Israel's privileged relationship with God was fully realized, and Christ was

1

incensed at what he regarded as the lack of reverence for the temple reflected by debased religious system."[1]

The temple in the Old Testament and the church in the New Testament are what Christ came to restore in accord with the original purpose of the Temple of God. Davidson concludes: "Throughout His ministry, he spoke and acted and reflected God's presence, and he saw himself as commissioned by God to be not simply a reformer, boldly calling for spiritual renewal, but to be the embodiment of the means by which God would bring redemption to his people."[2]

THE THREE-FOLD OFFICE OF CHRIST

Christ's three offices were manifested in human history as the means to redeem His bride. Andrew Murray asserts:

> Jesus Christ as Prophet, Priest and King meets all three needs of my being. As Prophet, He brings the light of God into my heart. He reveals to me my sin and wretchedness. My sinfulness is the first thing He shows me in the light of my sin. He also tells me about God's love and the way to God. He tells me that His Father has made Him a Priest to bring me near to Him. Shining into my heart as a prophet, He brings me to His priestly work of redeeming, purging and sanctifying. He teaches me to understand the meaning of His work. You see the Prophet first, and then the Priest. Finally, comes, the kingly office. As King, He fits me to rule over sin and self.[3]

Murray and Flavel accurately summarize Christ's three-fold office as the head of the true church. The three-fold office of Christ is His

---

[1] Ivor, J. Davidson, *The Birth of the Church*, Vol. 1 (Grand Rapids: Baker Books Publishers, 2004), 13.

[2] Ibid., 13.

[3] Andrew Murray and John Flavel, *The Believer's Prophet, Priest and King*, (Minneapolis: Bethany House Publishers, 1989), 38.

means to reach out to the bride who is lost and to bring her back to Himself.

THE LESSONS FOR THE CHURCH TODAY: UNIVERSAL AND AFRICA

The church's inception before creation needs to be understood on the basis of Christ's foreknowledge of the elect. The three-fold office of Christ was designed before the creation of the world by God for redemption. The lessons derived from the doctrines and teachings of the church must stand the test of the day and must continue in her integrity, purity, and sanctity, learning from the church in history. The Catholic Church (universal) has the mandate to preach and to disciple all the nations as Christ commanded (Matt. 28:18-20). Acculturation, secularism, and syncretism pose a great threat to the universal church. One African theologian contends,

> We can trace Christ's ancestor-ship to us, primarily to our common originality. In this respect, Christ's messiah-ship and ancestor-ship become meaningful to us. Christ's ancestor-ship is also grounded on his supernatural status. The supernatural status of the ancestors endows them with the supernatural powers and qualities that enable them to mediate between God and people.[4]

Some African scholars have corrupted the doctrine of the deity of Christ and regard Him in line with their belief of an ancestor who mediates on their behalf in a spirit-medium position or office. This research study will address that phenomenon critically.

The Triune God pre-planned the church before creation for the salvation of man. Christ is the head of the church and was incarnated in order to redeem her from her sins. The church started in the Old

---

[4] C., Nyamiti, *Christ Our Answer, Christology from an African Perspective*, (Gweru: Mambo Press, 1984), 19.

Testament after creation and was augmented in the New Testament but the inception, i.e. the initial plan was before creation because Christ is eternal. The church fathers have taught the need for the church to remain vigilant, pure from apostasy, and holy for the glory of God. The doctrines that the Reformers formulated have helped the church thrive and continue to do so in the 21st century. The universal church in general and African church in particular, should guard herself from secularism, syncretism, heresy, and apostasy.

ORGANIZATION

The research study will address, examine and suggest answers to many questions about the concept of the inception of the true church before with Christ in His three-fold office as prophet, priest, and king. The Reformers' contributions to the doctrines and the lessons for today's church will be articulated in order to enhance the understanding of the sound doctrines. In this context, this thesis will address, examine, and suggest the answers to questions as to the concepts about the inception of the church before creation.

The thesis will be structured into six chapters. Chapter One will include the introduction. The chapter will start with the introduction of the inception of the church. The question to be answered is, was the inception of the church in the Old Testament, in the New Testament, or before creation? The three-fold office of Christ will be discussed. When and how did He become Prophet, Priest and King? The purpose of the offices will be answered in this section. The Reformers' contributions to the church will be discussed extensively about the church's, doctrines, teachings, and practices. Key terms will be defined in brief in order to understand the subject matter of the subtopics. The background of the study will be outlined to give the fundamental reasons for choosing this topic. The purpose of this research study will be explained in detail. The chapter will end by giving the Thesis Statement.

Chapter Two consists of the literature review in historical context. The chapter will review the related literature of the topic and subtopics. Some of the authors who wrote on the subject will be examined. The assertion that the church was incepted before creation to eternity will be elaborated up on. The church in various periods, with some its prominent theologians, will be examined, including the early church during Simon Peter; the Patristic Period with St. Augustine of Hippo; medieval period with Thomas Aquinas; the Reformation with John Calvin; the Post-Reformation with John Bunyan; and the Evangelical Movement with George Whitefield, a Calvinist and John Wesley, an Arminian. The chapter examines the historical background of the church to highlight how these above mentioned figures defended and played pivotal roles in how the is to be viewed.

Chapter Three will examine the biblical understanding of the church. What does the Bible say about the church being conceived before creation? The following doctrines will be discussed in this chapter: election, predestination, redemption, adoption, and the meaning of a visible and an invisible church. The meaning of the true church and its marks will be articulated.

Chapter Four will discuss the three-fold office of Christ. Christ as Prophet, Priest and King will be discussed from both Old and New Testament perspectives. These three offices of Christ were Godly means of reaching out to save His bride, the church.

Chapter Five will discuss practical issues of the universal church, and the African church in particular. The African church is characterized by acculturation and syncretism while the Western church is characterized by secularism and materialism. The chapter will deal with the true African church and the emerging churches that have deceived and distorted the church of Christ in Africa.

Chapter Six summarizes and concludes the thesis. Throughout, analysis and exegetical examinations of the words and history will be discussed to enhance the understanding of the context.

BACKGROUND

Research that has been done by other scholars on this subject often does not give substantial answers to the question of the inception of the church before creation. Christ manifested Himself as head of the church as Prophet, Priest, and King. The research that has been done, good as it may be, often has not answered the fundamental questions and issues concerning the inception of the church before creation. Most research does not blend the inception of the church with Christ as the head of the church nor does it address why and how Christ manifested himself as prophet, priest and king. This thesis will answer the questions about the inception of the church and the three-fold offices of Christ and will define the meaning of the universal church. It will also provide some detail about the church in Africa and particularly in Zimbabwe.

The contributions of church leaders, and other theologians helped to shape the church. John Calvin serves as a good example of one of the renowned Reformers who guarded, defended, and taught the true doctrines of the church. The church in Africa is threatened by all kinds of acculturation, syncretism, and apostasy. There is a great need to have a comprehensive doctrine about the inception of the church and the relationship of the church to Christ and His three offices. The gaps that other research studies do not address will be answered in this thesis. This will provide insights regarding the inception of the church and the purposes of the three-fold office of Christ. It will provide Christian critical thinking. The research will allow Christians to appreciate the vast plans that God has for His elect. As a result, the church will celebrate and worship the sovereign God for all His mercy bestowed on the church before creation.

The heritage of the doctrines of the church must be preserved for equipping the church and must be passed on because they are the foundation of the church in Christ. Christ and the church are inseparable. Christ's offices as prophet, priest and king hinge on Him as the head of the church forever. The invisible church did not start at creation or with men, nor after the fall but before creation. The church was in the mind of the Godhead from before the foundation of the world (Eph. 1:4 14). The church is eternal because Christ, the head of the church is eternal.

■ CHAPTER 2 ■

THE CHURCH'S INCEPTION HISTORICALLY

OLD TESTAMENT

The Greek term for church *ekklesia,* literally means "called out." The term signifies the body of believers who have been saved by Christ through faith in Him. The church is signified and typified after the fall when God sought after Adam to restore Him back to his original relationship with God. God called out to Adam, "And the Lord God called unto Adam, and said unto him, Where art thou?" (Gen. 3:9). Adam responded by coming out and confessing what he had done. In fact, Adam blamed the woman and the woman blamed the serpent. No one wanted to own the responsibility of sin (Gen. 3:12-13). Nevertheless, God clothed them with an animal skin, signifying the blood of Christ to take away the sin of the world.

Cain and Abel brought their offering unto the Lord. God accepted Abel's offering of the firstlings of his flock and of the fat thereof and rejected Cain's, the fruit offering of the ground unto the Lord (Gen. 4:4-5). This resembles the church whereby God chooses some and rejects other on His merit. God accepted the offering of an animal sacrifice from Abel with the foreknowledge that His Son will atone and be a ransom for those many who would believe in Him. My assumption is that the fruit Cain offered was rejected it was unholy, providing no means of atonement. When men had become wicked in the eyes of God, He planned to destroy them with the flood. But God was merciful and gracious to Noah because Noah was upright and righteous. "And the LORD said unto Noah, Come thou and thy entire house into the ark; for thee I have seen righteous before me in this generation" (Gen. 7:1). Noah's family was saved while the whole earth was destroyed by water. This example illustrates the election by God calling out some and rejecting others. Esau was rejected while Jacob was chosen according to the story (Gen. 25:19-34). The doctrine of election, predestination, and adoption are God's design initiated before creation. As human history unfolds, from one generation to another, God calls out His chosen ones, thus *ekklesia*.

The church is the body of believers, the bride of Christ, Him being the bridegroom and the head. Then the question arises, when did the Church start? Did it start in the Old Testament, in the New Testament or before creation? Some assert the church started in the Old Testament. Others suggest that the church started in the New Testament at Pentecost when the Jews and the proselytes gathered to celebrate the Pentecost. However, if Christ is eternal as the head of the church, the institution of the church is eternal because Christ cannot be the head of a temporary institution. The underlying factor is that the eternal Christ was incarnated for the sake of sinners needing redemption because of the fall of Adam. After His resurrection, Christ continued in His divine nature, being the head of the church even today and forever. He will continue to be head of the church. All believers will live forever after the resurrection. The argument does not suggest that believers are or were eternal before creation. But that they will live eternal life with Christ Jesus. How does He continue to be the head of the church?

There are two schools of thought about the inception of the church. The view of the first school of thought states that,

> The people of Israel believed that they had a special
> relationship with their God, YAHWH. They tried to
> understand and explain the nature of this relationship
> through the metaphor of marriage. They even tried

to interpret their history in terms of this theme and to foresee their future history through this. Needless to say, the major theme such as election, covenant, rejection and restoration found in the Old Testament are some of the ways used to explain the relationship.... The metaphor of marriage is one of the typical means used to portray the relationship between YHWH and Israel in the Old Testament along with the metaphors of father-son, shepherd-sheep, king-royal servants, general-soldier, master-slave, farmer-vineyard, etc. In the New Testament not only does Jesus use this metaphor in order to proclaim himself as God as well as the Messiah promised in the Old Testament, but also many of the biblical writers use the same metaphor to explain the relationship between Christ and his church.[5]

This school of thought defends the position that Israel was God's chosen nation. God chose to demonstrate and to represent His intimate relationship with her, to love her and to be her God forever. As a result, YHWH made a covenant with Israel through a promise to Abraham. The previous covenant made with Adam is part of the covenant of works, which was broken. This school of thought asserts that Israel was the type of church in the Old Testament, although it was just one nation. However, it represented the future church.

The metaphor of marriage in the history of Israel dates back to the worship and service to YHWH as their God. They regarded themselves as the wife and YHWH as the husband; hence faithfulness, honesty, love, and intimate relationship were not options but obligations, especially on the side of the wife who should submit herself to the husband as the head of the household. The prophets, Hosea, Jeremiah, and Ezekiel compared the relationship of YHWH with Israel as husband and wife. Hosea dramatized the marriage in the practical sense when he married a harlot. Michael Eaton gives us a glimpse of the assertion of this drama:

---

[5] Seock-Tae Sohn, *YHWH: the Husband of Israel* (Eugene: Wipf and Stock Publishers, 2002), 1.

Hosea was a young man, loyal to the faith of the house David in the south, and aged in his middle twenties when he was called to be a prophet. However, the marriage of Hosea is a matter of dispute. As described in Hosea chapter 1, Hosea's marriage has been taken in at least the following four ways. 1. There was a time when Hosea 1:2 was widely taken to refer to a vision or a parable rather than an actual event. 2. Others have assumed that every girl in northern Israel was guilty of immorality because the pagan religion of the land. Hosea was simply marrying a typical northern Israelite. 3. Others understand it to mean that Hosea was called to marry a 'cult prostitute', a temple-prostitute who had been involved in the immorality of the pagan rites of north Israel. 4. Another view is that Hosea took a woman whom he thought would be pure only to find out later that she was immoral. Hosea then discovered the purpose of God in what had happened to him. On this view, 'woman of harlotry' either means 'woman with immoral tendencies' or the narrative is projecting into the past what only became obvious later.[6]

Israel was a chosen nation by YHWH, to demonstrate His love to all the nations that God, the creator, is a God of relationships, as is exemplified in the First Commandment: "Thou shalt not have other gods before me. (Exodus 20:3)" In this incident, God wanted his prophet, Hosea, to experience this painful and traumatic marriage in his life in order to feel the burden of spiritual unfaithfulness of His chosen wife, Israel. "And the Lord said to Hosea, go, take unto thee a wife of whoredoms and children of whoredoms: for the land hath committed great whoredom, departing from the Lord, (Hosea 1:2b)."

Marriage is the deepest union possible between two people. It is the most intensely personal relationship that there is. It involves feelings, emotions, and perhaps,

---

[6] Michael A. Eaton, *Focus on Hosea* (Fearn: Christian Focus, 1996), 14.

resentments and jealousies. It is joining together of interest and concerns. It is loyalty. If a wife or a husband says one word against the other in public, the other feels betrayed. What then is spiritual adultery? It is broken conversation. It is when God is no longer listening or speaking to his people. It is prayerlessness. It is broken loyalty. It is fractured and dissevered channels of fellowship. There is no pain like the pain of disloyalty within marriage, and in Hosea's day this was the way God felt about Israel.[7]

Israel had abandoned God thus committing harlotry. They committed sin and violated the first of the Ten Commandments. They had turned to the Canaanite gods; they had turned to robbery and turned to violence. The leadership and the priests, the prophets, the kings were wicked and never consulted God any more. They had plunged into idolatry, immorality, drunkenness, fornication, and had become spiritually ruined. This spiritual adultery was detested by God.

I concur with this first school of thought which asserts that Israel is the representative of the New Testament church. As the sacrifices of animals and their blood cleansed the sins of the people foreshadowed Christ's atoning the nation of Israel in the Old Testament so the shadow of the universal church in the New Testament was sealed by the Holy Spirit at Pentecost. The inception of the invisible church was therefore before creation and the realization of the universal and visible church was in the Old Testament and subsequently in the New Testament.

The church is an institution founded on Christ for the salvation of humankind. Those who contend that the church was embedded in Israel believe that Abram was the first "called out" the first ekklesia. The promise came to Abraham by God, "I will multiply thy seeds as the stars of the heaven and as the sand which is upon the sea shore (Gen. 22:17)." The promise of Abraham was the promise of the church in the Old Testament (Israel) which would be the shadow of the New Testament church. In Galatians 3:6-14, Paul presents a fascinating discussion of

---

[7] Ibid., 28.

the differences between two covenant-administrations, one made with Abraham and another made with Israel at Sinai 430 years later.

Paul understood the covenant with Abraham to include essentially three promises: that God would give Abraham numerous descendents (and his seeds), the land of Canaan, and that God would bless all the nations of the world through Abraham and his seed. Plainly enough, the Israelites became numerous during their four hundred years in Egypt, and through Joshua and Judges, they inherited the land of Canaan. But they did not become the means by which all the Gentiles were blessed until the calling of Paul. Arguably, as long as the Sinai covenant distinguished Jew from Gentile, the seed of Abraham could not become a blessing to all nations. That is, the terms of the Sinai administration itself, being made with one peculiar nation and excluding others through dietary and ceremonial laws, prevented the entire fulfillment of the Abrahamic promise, even while it preserved memory of that promise and even while it preserves the integrity of Abraham's "seed" by prohibiting intermarriage with Gentiles.[8]

Some scholars believe that at Mount Sinai, the church of the Old Testament was incepted, "In the Exodus narrative structure surrounding the giving of the Law on Mount Sinai, the Ten Commandments follow almost immediately Moses' proclamation that Israel is the prized possession of God and is to be a kingdom of priests and a holy nation."[9]

When Hosea dramatized the apostasy of Israel by marrying the harlot Gomer, God was demonstrating that the church should not be defiled by committing adultery, worshiping the idols as the nation of Israel had done. James Bannerman asserts that,

> I do not stop to inquire into the nature and exercise of
> this ordinance under the Old Testament Church, as it
> would require a lengthened discussion in order to do

---

[8] Bryan D. Estelle, J. V. Fesko and David Van Drunen, *The Law is not Faith* (Phillipsburg: P & R Publishing House, 2009), 421.

[9] David Filbeck, *Yes, God of the Gentiles, Too*, (Wheaton: Zondervan Publishing House, 1994), 70.

justice to the subject. But I may say that nothing seems more certainly susceptible of proof than that, apart from any exercise of civil authority on the side of the state, there was also an exercise of ecclesiastical authority in the Jewish Church, in the way of depriving transgressors of the privileges of the Church, and excluding them from the congregation in Divine worship.[10]

The nation of Israel was indeed a Jewish church. She was a nation of God's chosen people whom God wanted to single out to demonstrate to all the nations how much He loved and cared for her. "Election refers to an exclusive relationship between Yahweh and the people of Israel. Yahweh's choice of Israel is a part of this relationship. The main concern of election in the Bible is not in reference to a past event when Yahweh chose Israel as his people."[11] God showed His love to Israel to demonstrate the manner in which He loves the universal church.

The church is "called out" ekklesia, the people of God called out to worship Him in truth and in spirit. The nation of Israel was a Jewish church. John Owen states that,

There was a twofold defection of the Jewish Church from this new phase of theology-first, a partial apostasy which was healed by a new effusion of the grace of God; and, later, a further rebellion which issued in the total destruction of that people as its punishment. The later ruin was more swiftly hastened after the Church was divided into two-one part consisting of ten tribes, and the other holding the seat of solemn worship instituted by God Himself. So great an apostasy of the Jewish Church can only have come about through rejection of those foundational theological truths.[12]

---

[10] James Bannerman, *The Church of Christ Vol. II* (Edinburgh: The Banner of Truth Trust, 1960), 190.

[11] Seock-Tae Sohn, *The Divine Election of Israel* (Grand Rapids: William B. Eerdmans Publishing House, 1991), 4.

[12] John Owen, *Biblical Theology* (Morgan: Soli Deo Gloria, 1994), 439.

The church in the Old Testament, which was composed of one nation, Israel, as God's chosen people, did not fulfill the promise and the covenant. Israel broke the covenants and committed adultery. John Owen contends that, "The eventual outcome would demonstrate that God had not abandoned his care for his church during the years of captivity, and during it his prophetic promises continued to inspire the faith of the pious."[13] Owen reiterates that the nation of Israel was the church, "By such means were laid the foundations of the reformed Jewish church, on her return from Babylonian captivity."[14] It is fundamentally true that the church existed in the Old Testament and the nation of Israel was a church though not yet complete. As a symbol of the church, she was composed of but one nation. The church was patterned and fashioned according to God's design.

After the fall of Adam and Eve, we encounter the first justification of Abel. The chronicles of justification, redemption and sanctification in the Old Testament unveils throughout the human history from Adam, Enoch, Noah, Abraham, Lot, Isaac, Jacob, Joseph and Moses. These were "called-out" leaders who were to lead subsequently, the people of God. The nation of Israel, the church in the Old Testament, was redeemed from Egypt to worship God in the desert, (Ex. 3:10; 5:1). The redemption of Israel from Egypt is symbolic of the redeemed church of Jesus Christ from the world. Israel saw herself as God's chosen nation although once in a while plunged into idolatry. Israel and Lebar asset,

> In the first century the Jewish people were neither a nation founded on the Graeco-Roman ideal nor, *a fortiori*, a nation in the present-day sense of the term, with an individual history and its natural interests to defend. The Jewish people believed they were chosen by God, as a 'kingdom of priests and a holy people.' Moreover, the Holy of Holies and, by extension, the entire Temple and Jerusalem itself were not a capital city, a national symbol, a seat of government, but a place in which the Divine Presence was manifest. Thus one

---

[13] Ibid., 489.
[14] Ibid., 493.

of God's names retained by Jewish tradition is *Makom,* which is a Hebrew word meaning place, spot, particular point.[15]

One can therefore assume that Israel knew who they were and that God was their God. Worship instituted by God is for His own good pleasure.

Israel was very much aware of her identity but little did she know that she was a representative of the church of Jesus Christ. She kept defiling herself with idol worship. "This, then, was the defection of the church which God was pleased, in His great long suffering, to purge out by the chastisement of the 70 years captivity....The apostasy of the church within Judah, being almost but not quite total, thus met a deserved and terrible end. Jerusalem itself and the Temple were laid waste by fire and sword and leveled to the ground.... And yet God had not exhausted His patient love for His people, nor His providential care for His church."[16] History reveals that God had not abandoned His church, the Jewish church during the years of captivity. He needed to reform the church into the shape He intended her to be in His original plan.

Owen states that after the Israel's restoration, "The church was purified by putting away of strange wives, and foreign wives who had gradually been intermingled with the people from the days of Solomon onward, destruction of idolatry and immorality laying out the foundation of the reformed Jewish church."[17] Owen puts it so passionately when he says, "I pray that God will allow no one else in the future of the church to so reproach his care, providence and love towards his church!... It is just this. when the prophetic ministry came to an end in the

Jewish church that there at once, arose a responsibility to preserve the Scriptures in their purity."[18] Owen strongly believed in the existence of the Jewish church in the Old Testament. The Septuagint described that the Jewish church was crumbling to complete defection in the Old

---

[15] Gerard Israel and Jacques Lebar, *When Jerusalem Burned* (New York: William Morrow & Company, 1973), 20.

[16] Ibid., 489.

[17] Ibid., 493.

[18] Ibid., 495.

Testament. However, God always shapes His church in His own pattern and preserves her. As He intervened in the building of the Temple with David, Nathan and Solomon, He directs it even today.

Although David says he received the plans for the temple from YHWH (I Chronicles 28:19), the narratives emphasize David's initiative and make no reference to his involvement in the project. After David and Nathan first devise a building plan, YHWH intervenes to express an opinion on the matter and to outline some hesitations (2 Sam. 7:4-7). Back at Sinai it was YHWH who took the initiative in commissioning a place to dwell among the Israelites and a place to meet with them, and the place YHWH commissioned was emphatically mobile. The wilderness tent contrasted with the gold calf Aaron built while YHWH was giving the specifications for the tent, but it also contrasts with the city palace for YHWH that David planned."[19]

First Chronicles shows us that God's story of Israel with David as her king predicts God's involvement with the entire world in human history. In the dedication of Solomon's Temple, Solomon's prayer sermon incorporated all races, languages, ethnics, tribes, and all the peoples of the world as envisioning the nature of Christ's church by the Holy Spirit (2 Chron. 6:4-42). In verse 32 Solomon incorporates foreigners into the blessings of God when they enter into the temple to pray to YHWH. The mindset that the temple would be the universal church found its way into the hearts of the leaders of Israel.

NEW TESTAMENT

In the New Testament, the prophecy given in Isaiah 7:14, "Therefore the Lord himself shall give you a sign; Behold, a virgin shall conceive, and bear a son, and shall call his name Immanuel." In Hebrew, Emmanuel means God with us. It is a theophonic name used in Isaiah 7:14 and Isaiah 8:8. It appears only once in the New Testament and is quoted only by Matthew. Immanuel is the prophesied Messiah. The Gospels provide narration of the birth of Christ, His ministry, His death and

---

[19] John Goldingay, *Old Testament Theology*, Vol. 1 of Old Testament Theology (Downers Grove: Intervarsity Press, 2003), 563.

resurrection, and His ascension. The main purpose of the incarnate Christ was to redeem the church, His bride. Christ connects the Old Testament with the New Testament. He is the pivot of both the old and then the new era in the history of the church. The redemptive history of the church is always focused on Christ because the church is born of Christ. Alfred Edersheim states:

> Among the outward means by which the religion of Israel was preserved, one of the most important was the centralization and localization of its worship in Jerusalem....Whenever a Roman, a Greek, or an Asiatic might wander, he could take his gods with him, or find rites kindred to his own. It was far otherwise with the Jew. He had only one Temple, that in Jerusalem; only one God, Him who had once been throned there between the Cherubim, and who was still King over Zion.[20]

The heavens delighted in the incarnation of Christ to redeem the world and to save it as the scriptures declare. The concept of incarnation should be understood clearly because it is the cradle of redemption, justification, sanctification, and glorification.

Without the incarnation, there would be no salvation at all; hence there would be no visible church, as it were. The connection between the old era and the new era of church history is built on Christ. Solomon and Herod each built a temple. The temple that Solomon built was the last church of the Old Testament and the temple which Herod built was the first of the New Testament era, but subsequently, Christ built the everlasting Temple, which is the church that He inaugurated in the New Testament, beginning with the choosing of the twelve disciples. Charles Spurgeon puts the incarnation of Christ beautifully when he says,

> The reservoir of time had been filled by the inflowing of age after age; and when it was full to the brim, the Son appeared. Why the world should have remained without

---

[20] Alfred Edersheim, *The Life and Times of Jesus the Messiah* (Grand Rapids: Wm B. Eerdmans, 1981), 3.

Him who is its one great light for four thousand years after Adam was formed out of the dust of the earth, and why it should have taken that length of time for the Jewish Church to attain her full age, we cannot tell; but this we are plainly told, that Jesus was sent forth 'when the fullness of the time was come.' Our Lord did not come before His time, nor behind His time; He was punctual to the appointed hour, and cried, to the exact moment, 'Lo, I come.'[21]

Christ's coming on earth was the fulfillment of all the prophecies about Immanuel, who was to take away the sins of the world. His incarnation was misunderstood, and continues to be misunderstood and misinterpreted but the fact remains the same: God became flesh and dwelt among His people but the people did not comprehend Him as John declares.

Arthur Custance summarizes the concept of incarnation so fittingly. When Jesus came down from His glory to become man, a new relationship was established with His Father and He became a Son. When Christ was incarnated, the main purpose was to redeem the bride who was deceived and lost in sin. He humbled Himself to reach out for her. He connected the Old Testament prophesies, that which predicted His coming, and the New Testament, which was the fulfillment of the prophecies. The seed which was promised Abraham is Christ (Gal. 3:16), and the Seed is sinless. The Seed which was sown is incorruptible (1 Pet. 1:23) for it is Christ. The church is born in Christ and by Christ. Robert Wilberforce asserts that, "On this intimate relation between the Head and the members between Him who entered the human family, that He might not exhibit its capacities in their highest state, but bestow upon it gifts of which it was before incapable depends on the efficacy of what Christ effected for man's nature in His death, and of what He 'ever liveth' to the effect for it through His intercession.... Our Lord was

---

[21] Charles H. Spurgeon, *Christ's Incarnation* (Pasadena: Pilgrim Publications, 1978), 23.

the Pattern Man, the second Adam-First, by office; second by Nature; thirdly, by Sympathy."[22]

The church began in the New Testament with the birth of Christ. Jesus confirmed Himself as the foundation of the church in Matthew 16:18, "And I say also unto thee, That thou art Peter, and upon this rock I will build my church; and the gates of hell shall not prevail against it." Peter, in Greek (*petros, masc.*), signifies a stone or fragments of rock; our Lord being the STONE, (*petra, fem.*). Christ is called a rock (Isa. 28:16, 1 Pet.2:8). Because of a change in the Greek word, many conservative scholars believe that Christ is building the church on Himself. Some scholars contend that Christ is building the church on Peter and the other apostles as the building's foundation stones (Eph. 2:20; Rev. 21:4). Still other scholars propound that the church is built on Peter's confession or testimony. Rabbinical scholars understood that when the Old Testament referred to a rock, it represented God. God is the rock and His work is perfect, immovable and solid (Deut. 32:4).

In Matthew 16:18 is the first mention of the word church in the New Testament. In Greek the word is *ekklesia*, literally meaning a "called-out assembly." The word is used in the New Testament 114 times. What Peter confessed includes all the people who believe and confess Christ as Lord. The church of Christ is being fully realized and recognized in the New Testament.

After denying Christ three times, Peter was asked by Jesus whether he loved Him (John 21:15-17). Peter could not deny he did. Three times Christ commissioned him to feed His sheep. Loving Christ and feeding his flock goes hand in hand. The church is the bride of Christ and He loves her dearly. Anyone who takes care of and feeds the flock, the church, first he should fall in love with Christ because when one looks at the church, he sees Christ in her, His love, His redemption, His sanctification and His glorification. The entire package of Christ and His solution is embraced in His church. "Feed my lambs" here means to care for the flock by furnishing nourishment. The Greek word is βόσκε i.e. 'feed,' the flock. In verse 16, the Greek word ποίμαινε, 'feed'

---

[22] Robert Isaac Wilberforce, *The Doctrine of the Incarnation of Our Lord Jesus Christ in its Relationship to Mankind and to the Church* (Philadelphia: H. Hooker, 1849), 27.

changes to denote the care, guidance, and protection of the sheep by a shepherd. It is therefore implied that our Lord Jesus was teaching that the shepherd was to feed the flock with proper food and also to govern her according to the Word of God. In verses, 15 and 16, the word love φίλώ is the same. Christ has entrusted the church to His faithful ones.

As time progresses, we observe Peter shaping the church although at first he was reluctant to incorporate the Gentiles into the early church. Then God showed him a vision, and in the vision, a voice said to him, "Rise, Peter; kill and eat....What God hath cleansed, that call not thou common" (Acts 10:13, 14). The vision was to tell Peter that God does not discriminate on the basis of race or nationality but that His grace extends beyond the Jews. Peter and Paul were the first prominent figures who set up the biblical standards as to how the Christians could conduct themselves in relation to circumcision, food, worship and dress, as well in relating to the world. The church of Christ in the early church multiplied and she served Christ Himself.

The following sections are fundamentally important in outlining the prominent figures in church history who tried to preserve, guard, and defend Christianity in their times. Each section does not answer diversity the question about the inception of the church but they do show how God preserved of the ancient church. They are important to highlight how apostasies and heresies meant to thwart the doctrines and the expansion of the church were overcome. Such heresies were challenged and defeated in the name of Jesus Christ, the head of the church. The church grew from one period to another in its stance, faith, and resilience against all forms of oppositions. These sections will underscore the importance of God's grace working through these men who did not shrink back or retreat but stood on biblical principles, by faith, to defend the church of Jesus Christ.

PATRISTIC PERIOD: AUGUSTINE

The progression of the events from the Old Testament to the New Testament gradually sheds light on the promise of God to Abraham about his seed and the inauguration of the kingship of David. Alec

Motyer propounds that "The Old Testament does not make it clear by what steps this hope moved from longing for a better ruler to the expectation of the perfect ruler. The beginnings of hope are firmly set in the days of David by the foundational oracles of Nathan in 2 Samuel 7 yet it promises no more than an endless Davidic line, ever under the blessing of the Lord. 'Your house and your kingdom shall endure for ever before me; your throne shall be established for ever' (2 Sam. 7:16)."[23] The prophecies and the fulfillment of the promises of God are inevitable and come to pass all the time as predicated by the Holy Scriptures. The promised seed, the second Adam would come to inaugurate the church and the bride for ever for Christ.

Many scholars contend that the church began at Pentecost. "In 38 AD, the first great Christian community was founded in pagan surroundings, at Antioch in Syria, 620 kilometers north of Jerusalem.... The first advantage is that the Christian religion did not present itself as a new religion. It was the very same religion of Yahweh which was revealed formerly to Abraham and to the prophets and which tended wholly toward the Messiah."[24] There is continuity between Israel in the Old Testament and the church in the New Testament. Verbraken reiterates "Let us remember that the Jewish religion was reserved in practice to the Jewish people, to the descendants of Abraham; the Christian message, however, was addressed to all men without discrimination."[25] We know from the Scriptures that the church was founded by Jesus Christ and we know that He established it on the foundation of the apostles.

When did the church really start? Those scholars who assert that the church began at the day of Pentecost have stated that the coming down of the Holy Spirit was a sign and a seal of the inception of the church. I concur with the assertion that the church began at the day of Pentecost in the New Testament period, but the initial inception was before creation. I also agree with those scholars who say Israel was the type of the church in the Old Testament. To trace the beginnings of the church on earth is imperative. As we have seen, the church existed

---

[23] Alec Motyer, *Look to the Rock* (Grand Rapids: Kregel Publications, 1996), 30.
[24] Patrick Verbraken, *The Beginnings of the Church* (New York: Paulist Press, 1968), 1.
[25] Ibid., 2.

in the Old Testament; now we are tracing its continuance in the New Testament. Jesus gave to His disciples the authority they needed to lead the church on His behalf. With His questions, Jesus delegated authority to St. Peter after His resurrection when He told him three times to feed His sheep (John 21:15-19).

The feast of Pentecost was celebrated fifty days after the Passover (Acts 2:1-13). It commenced on the fiftieth day, reckoned from the first day of the unleavened bread (Lev. 23:15-16). The feast was instituted as a commemoration of the giving of the Law by God at Mount Sinai to the people of Israel and Moses who was the spokes man of God. "There is a correspondence between the giving of the Law, which is celebrated by this feast of Pentecost, together with the crucifixion of our Lord, which took place at the Passover and this descent of the Holy Spirit, which happened at Pentecost. At Pentecost, God gave his Law on Mount Sinai, accompanied with thundering and lightning. On Pentecost, God sent down his Holy Spirit, like a rushing mighty wind; and tongues of fire sat upon each disciple, in order that, by His influence, that new law of light and life might be promulgated and established."[26]

Everyone who was Pentecost heard the apostles speak in his own language. The countries and areas mentioned are Pasthia, Media, Elam, Mesopotamia, Judea, Cappadocia, Pontus, Asia, Phrygia, Pamphylia, Egypt, Lybia, Cyrene, Rome, Crete, and Arabia. There was diversity of peoples and languages. Africa, Asia, and the Europe were represented at the Day of the Pentecost. That inaugurated a new era of the church in the New Testament which was composed of all peoples of the world, unlike the Jewish church. That marked the birth of the New Testament church as recorded in the book of Acts. From thence, the church moved on to all parts of the world.

Nathan's prophesy fulfilled Davidic descendent as the inheritor of the Abrahamic 'seed.' To trace the foundation of the church in church history, we need to examine how the church came to fruition over the centuries. The Patristic period is outlined by C. Matthew McMahon in this fashion:

---

[26] James C. Gray and George M Adams, *Gray & Adams' Clarke Bible Commentary* Vol. 5 of Gray & Adams' Clarke Bible Commentary (Grand Rapids: Zondervan Publishing House, 1903), 263.

The Patristic Period is a vital point in the history of Christianity since it contextualizes the early Christian information from the time of the death of the last Apostle (John) (which runs roughly about 100 A.D. to the Middle Ages (451 A.D. and the Council of Chalcedon). It describes the cohesion between Judaism and Christianity and various theological points being sorted out. Most denominations find this period of church history vitally important on a similar scale. From Roman Catholicism to the Reformed Churches following Zwingli and Calvin, many basic Christian concepts are birthed during this age, which, for good reason, the church would continue to believe for all time as orthodox over and against all heretical sectaries. During the first two hundred years of this era the church was under persecution from various Roman emperors. It was heightened and at its worse with Diocletian (303 A.D.) who even persecuted his own wife and daughter for being Christians. Christianity became legalized as a religion in the era of Constantine (321 A.D.) which was the opposite side of the spectrum in relation to previous persecution. Various cities and geographical areas became of chief importance. The city of Alexandria emerged as a center of Christian theological education. The city of Antioch also became a leading center of Christian thought. Western North Africa gave birth to such men as Tertullian, Cyprian of Carthage, and Augustine of Hippo. The Patristic period is filled with theological importance on the development of Christian doctrine.[27]

Augustine is one of the pillars in church history and he is an embodiment of all ages. He lived when the Roman Empire was beginning to crumble. He was imbued with Graeco-Roman culture. He became the great theologian who shaped the theological structure of church

---

[27] Matthew C. McMahon, *A Puritan Mind*, website Maven, 2009.

doctrines which became pivotal in the early ecumenical councils of the church. Stan Grabowski says, "In Augustine, we find only the best of Graeco-Roman culture, but an embodiment of the Christian tradition of the first four centuries. The African Bishop stands in the middle of the patristic era like an immense reservoir, nourishing itself on many rivulets."[28]

Augustine was both the greatest theologian and the greatest philosopher of the patristic period. His brilliance in expounding the Holy Scriptures and made him a champion in fighting against heresies and schisms. Grabowski states: "No thinker, no philosopher, no religious writer outside the inspired authors of Sacred Scripture has enjoyed such a long, uninterrupted, unabated universal popularity in the Christian world as the unusual Saint of North Africa. He was and is the boast of the whole Christian Church the Protestant and the Catholic recognizes his genius and merit."[29]

Stan Grabowski goes on to say:

> St. Augustine sees Christ, the incarnate Word of God, identified with the Church. Not human wisdom but He alone is the Savior of men, the mediator between God and men, and she continues Christ's work on earth. She is the dispenser of life, the healer of human nature, the ark of salvation. She is the divinely appointed teacher in matters doctrinal and moral; her authority is unquestionable and surpasses that of the wisest of men. She governs and rules men in the name of God for their own good that they may attain supreme happiness in everlasting life.[30]

Augustine stood firm for the true church during his time. When the church was viewed at that time as failure and as a human institution Augustine stepped in to uphold the truth that the church was founded

---

[28] Stanislaus J. Grabowski, *The Church, An Introduction to the Theology of St. Augustine* (St. Louis: B. Herder Book Company, 1957), viii.

[29] Ibid., xi.

[30] Ibid., 1.

on Jesus Christ. Tim Dowley says, "Augustine's appointment as presbyter and Bishop of Hippo marked the beginning of a catholic resurgence, and hastened the downfall of the Donatists, who at their peak around 394 A.D. assembled 310 bishops.... Augustine stimulated the monastic movement within the Catholic church. Above all, Augustine raised the self-confidence and intellectual level of African Catholicism."[31]

The Donatists lived in the Roman province of North Africa in the fourth and fifth centuries. They were rigorists and held that the church must be composed of saints and not unconverted sinners. They believed that the sacraments such as baptism administered by *traditores* were invalid. But Augustine challenged that view saying that the church has both saints and unconverted sinners who both need the grace of God. He argued that even if the sacraments were administered by unconverted sinners, they were still valid. Augustine's influence dominated the medieval church in the West. Dowley notes: "Against the Donatists he insisted that the church was a mixed field of wheat and tares, believers and unbelievers, growing together until the harvest. He undercut Donatistic rebaptism by claiming that Christ is the chief minister of the sacraments, so that they remained true sacraments even if administered by unworthy people."[32] Augustine defended the purity of the church and shaped the church doctrines and orders amidst heresies, apostasy, and false doctrines that had crept into the church and were threatening to distort the true doctrines.

A.D.R. Polman says,

> St. Augustine saw Christ mainly as the eternal Word. The contemplation of this Word leads to knowledge of the truth and hence salvation. Here, Christ's incarnation was no more than precept and example, just as, in the attainment of a blessed life of contemplation, the Scriptures are no more than a starting point. And the preaching of God's Word is but a call to follow the glorious example of Christ. Then this attitude of St.

---

[31] Tim Dowley, *Introduction to the History of Christianity* (Minneapolis: Fortress Press, 2002), 205.
[32] Ibid., 210.

Augustine's gave way to one in which the philosophic interpretation of Christ as the Word still retained its value, but took its place side by side with the more scriptural interpretation, in which the Word was considered as the revelation of the Father, full of grace and truth. While St. Augustine always retained longing for the contemplation of God's truth and wisdom, his deeper understanding of man's sinfulness and blindness caused him to shift the stress to the role of Christ as Savior and to His great acts of salvation.[33]

Augustine stood out for the preservation of the church in the Patristic period and many of the doctrines that he formulated and maintained are still the heritage of the church.

MEDIEVAL PERIOD: THOMAS AQUINAS

The term 'medieval' comes from Latin meaning "middle age." This term wasn't introduced into English until the 19th century, a time when there was heightened interest in the art, history, and thought of the Middle Ages. There is some disagreement about when the Medieval Period started, whether it began in the 4th, or 5th, or 6th century A.D. Some scholars associate the beginning of the period with the collapse of the Roman empire, which began in 410 A.D. Scholars similarly disagree about when the period ends, whether they place the end at the start of the 15th century with the rise of the Renaissance Period, or in 1453 when Turkish forces captured Constantinople. The Middle Ages included the first sustained urbanization of northern and western Europe.

The most influential theologians who defended the church during the middle ages were Thomas Aquinas. "The waning influence of Thomism in the late medieval theology is sharply focused in the nominalist doctrine of God. Drawing on both biblical and traditional resources, an increasing number of voices were raised in rejection of Thomas's vision of God

---

[33] A.D.R. Polman, *The Word of God According to St. Augustine* (Grand Rapids: Eerdmans., 1961), 13.

as primarily intellect…. Will and intellect are distinct logically but not ontologically; indeed, 'will' and 'intellect' are but two of the ways in which it is proper to name God's essence when it is considered from different points of views…."[34] Thomas contended that God has freedom from any kind of external impingement. Thomas's doctrine of divine transcendence challenged heretics who wanted to compromise God's immanence in nature and history. He argues, "Will follows upon intellect; it is impossible for God to will anything but what his wisdom approves."[35]

The debates concerning God and creation raged in medieval nominalism, but Thomas Aquinas defended a high view of the church. He challenged those who claimed to reason from scientific logic about matter, God, and His attributes. He states, "Every material thing or substance is composed of a substantial form and first master. Neither principle is itself a thing or substance; the two together are the component principles of a substance. And it is only the substance that we can properly say that it exists."[36]

Thomas Aquinas argued with the philosophers of his time to show that the church should remain faithful. Timothy Renick asserts that:

> Thomas Aquinas ranks among the three or four most influential thinkers in the history of not merely Christianity but of Western thought in general. Aquinas's theory of natural law shaped our modern concept of human rights. His views of the state supplied the model for the argument of Thomas Jefferson in the Declaration of Independence. His commentaries on sex are still hugely influential. His views on the justice of warfare and the status on noncombatants have been

---

[34] John L. Farthering, *Thomas Aquinas and Gabriel Biel* (Durham: Duke University Press, 1988), 9.
[35] Ibid., 12.
[36] F.C. Copleston, *Aquinas* (Baltimore: Penguin, 1965), 90.

codified into international law and can be found in U.S. military handbooks.[37]

When Thomas Aquinas was born, Europe was recovering from the Dark Ages. The life of the mind was suppressed and church authority dominated. He should that human reason must be in subjection to God's wisdom and his sovereignty. Thomas challenged ideas and theology of Peter Abelard and Bernard. The Crusaders were bringing in strange new religious and intellectual ideas and the teachings of Islam. Aquinas rebutted those who were basing their arguments on blind faith and reason. He propounded that, "If the truths of the Bible and the truths of Christianity could be shown to have a rational basis for instance, if the existence of the Christian God could be shown to be not merely an article of faith and a claim asserted by the Bible but also a dictate of the reason. Then Christians could win the day against their new challengers. They could show their claims to be more than mere 'beliefs.' Christianity would become 'truth' mandated by reason."[38]

Aquinas thought that if Christianity was true it could be vindicated by reason. Some few people at that time doubted the credibility of Christianity and its claim that it held the truth. For some years the works of Aristotle had spread throughout the world and believed to be the only truth as he reasoned with logic, challenging the domain of Christianity. It posed to be dangerous and poisonous to Christian faith. Renick concludes that, "Whether or not you are Catholic, whether or not you are Christian, Aquinas has shaped the life you live, the ideas you hold, and the actions you perform. He changed the way we think about thinking and doing more to make intellectual pursuits respectable, even godly, than perhaps any other figure."[39]

---

[37] Timothy M. Renick, *Aquinas for Armchair Theologians* (Louisville: Westminster John Knox Press, 2002), 12.

[38] Ibid., 4.

[39] Ibid., 14.

REFORMATION PERIOD: JOHN CALVIN

Prominent figures in church history shaped the doctrines of the church of all ages. I will give more biographical information about John Calvin because he played a pivotal role as a Reformer and shaped the church in Geneva which became a model for the church. The Reformation did not start with John Calvin but he was one of the most influential Reformers. He taught and defended the sound doctrines of the church against heretics who wanted to pervert the Scripture to their own interpretations and understanding. His teachings and contributions to the church are an example of the great commitment to Scripture the Reformers had in defending and shaping church doctrines.

Henry Meeter summarizes John Calvin status and his position,

> John Calvin was born July 10, 1509. While Luther and Zwingli were contemporaries, Calvin belonged to the second generation of Reformers. At the time Luther posted 95 theses on the castle gate at Wittenberg on October 31, 1517, Calvin was only nine years old. In a sense, therefore, Calvin rested on the shoulders of the other two great reformers, but he nevertheless deserves a place next to them and is usually numbered as one of three great Protestant Reformers. The reason for this is that Calvin was the great organizer and systematizer of the ideas of the Reformation.[40]

John Calvin's father wanted him to be a priest; hence he encouraged him to go for priesthood between 1520 or in 1521. Joel Beeke says,

> About five years later, Calvin's father sent his son to Orleans to study law. This sudden, dramatic change of professions for young Calvin is noteworthy also for two reasons. First, Calvin's legal training fostered in him qualities of mind, clarity, precision, and caution that later served him well as Bible commentator and

---

[40] Henry Meeter, *The Life of John Calvin* (Grand Rapids: Calvin College, 1947), 3.

theologian. Second, the University of Orleans was where Calvin first came into contact with Reformation truth.[41]

John Calvin soon felt called to serve the Lord and that changed the entire church history. He shaped the church in Geneva in such a way that it would shape the entire universal church of Christ in later years. The doctrines that Calvin formulated and would help the church to stand against all forms of heresies that confronted the church in later centuries. In theology, Calvin demonstrated his deep understanding of each subject he addressed. Albert Hyma puts it this way,

> But all of a sudden he turned from legal studies to theology, from the things of this world to the kingdom of God. As a result, his first compositions dealt with religion. He approved of the work done by Erasmus only insofar as Erasmus urged people to return to the faith and morals of the early church. The Church needed reform, so said Erasmus. Luther said the same, but he produced the necessary action, while Erasmus merely produced literary compositions.[42]

John Calvin first published his Institutes when he was twenty-six years old.

John Calvin's theology has been embraced by many churches and has influenced many people to live and to serve the Lord according to the holy word of God. Joel Beeke asserts, "What a gift the church has in Calvin! Whether discussing economics, politics, ethics, theology, ecclesiology or domestic relation, I know of no man who helps the 21st century church more than John Calvin."[43] He stood out in the Reformation period and he is a true example of a Reformed and

---

[41] Joel R. Beeke, *"The Soul of Life": The Piety of John Calvin* (Grand Rapids: Reformation Heritage Books, 2009), 2.

[42] Albert Hyma, *The Life of John Calvin* (Grand Rapids: WM. B. Eerdmans, 1943), 27.

[43] Joel Beeke, *"Calvin for the 21st t Puritan Reformed Conference"* Grand Rapids, August 27-29, 2009.

experiential preacher. His doctrines shaped the church in Geneva and continue even today in the church.

POST-REFORMATION PERIOD: JOHN BUNYAN

Richard Greaves writes: "The Seventeenth Century, aptly referred to by historians as the century of revolution, was particularly an age of turmoil and change in England. Within that century no two decades witnessed more upheaval and revolutionary manifestation than those of 1640 to 1660.... Bunyan's life spanned that tumultuous period of English history extending from the Petition of Right of 1628 to the Glorious Revolution of 1688."[44] As Bunyan became a public speaker and engaged in public debates, especially with the Quakers, who relied on the Inner Light. This sparked a controversy when he insisted on the objective character of revelation.

Bunyan argued that Christ not only suffered death due to sinners (His passive obedience), but also that He perfectly fulfills the law. (His active obedience), for those same sinners, it was both this active and passive obedience that was necessary to satisfy divine justice."[45] Bunyan's teaching emphasized that the sinner ought to be assured by faith through the Scriptures that the love of God and the forgiveness of sins were guaranteed in Christ alone. He was a Puritan in his beliefs concerning faith, redemption, divine grace, election, and many sound doctrines that the Puritans upheld. Greaves says: "Bunyan was typically Calvinist regarding justification as acquittal and pronouncing of the sinner just."[46] Bunyan did extensive work in his writings, teaching Christians how they should conduct themselves. His books included Grace Abounding to the chief of Sinners, which is his spiritual autobiography, Pilgrim's Progress, The Holy War, and other treatises and sermons.

In ecclesiology, Bunyan was a Separatist. Roger Sharrock writes, "The sectarian impulse latent in Calvinism had first made itself during

---

[44] Richard L. Greaves, *John Bunyan* (Grand Rapids: Eerdmans, 1969), 13.
[45] Ibid., 39.
[46] Ibid., 77.

the political frustration of Puritanism under Elizabeth…The separatist conception of a church was a close voluntary association of believers."[47]

John Bunyan shaped the post-reformation Church. His writings have influenced many Christians on their spiritual pilgrimage. Sharrock asserts,

> The Pilgrim's Progress is one of the rare numbers of books which will always have readers, whether the pundits of literary taste should approve of it or not. It has, in fact, achieved an existence that is independent of literature; for the literary quality of a book is commonly weakened when it is translated into another language, but Bunyan's allegory has been translated into literally hundreds of dialects, and has maintained its appeal as a universal religious myth.[48]

Collmer comments: "At the tercentenary of John Bunyan's death, occasions present themselves to acclaim the author of the one book that has passed through more editions and into more foreign languages than any other book written in English."[49]

The Reformed churches have long recognized Bunyan's works. Monica Furlong notes:

"Nearly three hundred years after his death, John Bunyan is still a name known to many who are neither historians nor specialists in English literature. He is known principally as the author of The Pilgrim's Progress, and is paid perhaps the greatest compliment given to any author…"[50] Kenneth Dix assets that,

> If Bunyan had a high view of the pastoral office, he had an equally high view of a true Gospel Church. 'Church fellowship rightly managed is the glory of the

---

[47] Roger Sharrock, *John Bunyan* (New York: St. Martin's Press, 1968), 23.
[48] Ibid., 155.
[49] Robert G. Collmer, *Bunyan in our Time* (London: Kent State University Press, 1989), 1.
[50] Monica Furlong, *Puritan's Progress* (New York: Coward, McCann & Geoghegan, 1975), 13.

entire world. No place, no community, no fellowship, is adorned and bespangled with those beauties as is a church rightly knit together to their head, and lovingly serving one another; he said. 'No marvel then if this be the one thing that David desired, that which we seek after, to dwell in the House of the Lord all the days of his life. For Bunyan, that House of the Lord was not a building in Jerusalem or anywhere else, but the company of believers in and about Bedford, who in persecuting times met together as best they could, and whose records are still preserved.[51]

Bunyan influenced the church of his time, and he directed it the way she should go. Today, his teachings, doctrines, allegories, and books still continue to shape the church of Jesus Christ. He is one of the greatest figures in the Post-Reformation period.

EVANGELICAL PERIOD: GEORGE WHITEFIELD

George Whitefield was one of the principle figures in the Great Awakening of the early 1740s. The Great Awakening was a watershed event in the life of the American people. Before it was over, it had swept the colonies of the Eastern seaboard, transforming the social and religious life of the land. Whitefield is called the Great Itinerant. He was an associate of John Wesley in England in a very dark time for the church in England. Albert Belden writes: "If we are inclined on occasion to be depressed with the state of the Christian churches in our time, it may be of some encouragement to us to reflect that they are not nearly so sunken in depths of apathy and shame as was the church of the eighteenth century. That century was in many features both the worst and the best in our history."[52] George Whitefield was a man of his time,

---

[51] Kenneth Dix, *John Bunyan Puritan Pastor* (Rushden Northamptonshire: The Fauconberg Press, 1979), 5.

[52] Albert D. Belden, *George Whitefield-The Awakener* (London: Rock cliff Publishers, 1953), 53.

preaching in the open air and his voice was described as loud as a loud speaker. Whitefield expressed his zeal, convictions as follows:

> The doctrines of election, and free justification in Christ Jesus are daily more and more pressed upon my heart. They fill my soul with a holy fire and afford me great confidence in God my salvation. Put them in mind of the freeness and eternity of God's electing love...Press them to believe on Him immediately!...Speak every time, my dear brother, as if it was your last...[53]

Whitefield influenced the church and shaped it according to the Scriptures in the 18th century He is highly respected in Reformed and evangelical churches. He preached the 'True Gospel'. He was a Calvinist in doctrine and Puritan in preaching. His preaching and teaching brought about the Great Revival in America, working together with others. The evangelicalism spread rapidly and sunk its roots in the churches. The message of George Whitefield, has been summarized this way:

> He believed that the unchanging gospel is 'the power of God for all sorts of sinners' (Rom. 1:16). What was Whitefield's message? The doctrines known as Calvinism: the depravity of sinners and the freeness of God's grace; he rejoiced in the substitutionary atonement of Christ for God's elect; he proclaimed that all those for whom Christ died will persevere to the end of their lives and will then be glorified in heaven. Where did he learn these truths? 'My doctrines I had from Jesus Christ and His apostles; I was taught them of God', he wrote, and added two years later, 'I embrace the Calvinistic scheme, not because Calvin, but Jesus Christ, has taught it to me'. Whitefield, the convinced Calvinist, preached the gospel earnestly and

---

[53] Arnold A. Dallimore, *George Whitefield Vol. I* (Edinburgh: Banner of Truth Trust, 1989), 409.

persuasively urging and commanding sinners to go to Jesus Christ for salvation.[54]

Numerous sermons, public letters and journals were published during his lifetime and all affirm the integrity of George Whitefield as a Reformed, evangelist preacher.

CONCLUSION

The early church with St. Peter, as the prominent figure, ushered a new era of the church in the New Testament. Augustine fought against many heresies that were threatening the existence of the church. In the Middle Ages Thomas Aquinas defended the church and the existence of God.

John Calvin is one of the greatest theologians in church history. His teachings have saturated churches seminaries, universities, and the lives of the ordinary populace. His doctrines have guarded the church against threatening heresies. Calvinistic doctrines challenged Arminian doctrines until the present time. Calvinism has kept the sound doctrines of the Church. The post-Reformation period features John Bunyan standing against the heretics. He argued that Christ's death was due to sin and that Christ fulfilled the law perfectly. He said that both active and passive obedience were necessary to satisfy divine justice. During the period of the Great Awakening; George Whitefield continued to propagate Reformed truth. The Reformed churches held to Calvinistic views while the Liberals, Pentecostals, and other groups succumbed to Arminianism.

---

[54] Colin Thompson, "Revival Newsline: *The Reformation and Revival Fellowship*," *Journal of Revival Newsline, (Spring 2005): 569.*

CHAPTER 3

THE CHURCH'S INCEPTION BIBLICALLY

THE CHURCH'S INCEPTION BEFORE CREATION

This chapter will discuss at length that the church's inception was before creation. The church was a shadow in the Old Testament in the nation of Israel and then she was realized in the New Testament by the incarnation of Jesus Christ. She was sealed in the Day of Pentecost by the Holy Spirit. As such, it is fundamentally important to examine the inception of the church before creation within the Trinity. This chapter will also discuss the church before creation, i.e., the church having been incepted from the Godhead and then the doctrines of election, predestination, redemption, and adoption will be discussed also. The concept of a visible and invisible church will also be expounded in this chapter. The scriptures that confirm the doctrines of election, predestination, redemption, adoption, and eschatology will be examined.

Some scholars assert that the church began in the Old Testament. William Ramsay and John Leith ask, "When did the church begin? The answer depends partly upon what you mean by the question. But the basic answer is that the church began with creation of man. We must surely believe that God preserved, instructed, multiplied, honored, adorned, and called from death to life His Kirk (Church) in all ages since Adam.... As long as there has existed a believing fellowship of men with God, so long has the church existed."[55] God created man to live in fellowship with him. God revealed himself to men, not to animals or any other living being. God created man with the ability to befriend Him and to be loyal to his creator. But this phenomenon did not start with the creation of man but with Triune God. The Godhead had fellowship with Himself in three personalities: God the Father, God the Son, and God the Holy Spirit. The fellowship between God and man started after the creation. The perfect fellowship was ever in the Trinity and it will be there forever. Man rejected the fellowship with God by disobedience against God. Man's fall cut off fellowship with God.

The church on earth is designated as *ekklēsia* as 'gathering' or 'assembly' especially in the New Testament. Don Carson writes: "It is particularly significant that at the beginning of the two Corinthians letters…, the Church is described as belonging to the one who brought it into existence, that is, God, or a divinely created entity. Just as for Israel of old, the gatherings referred to by our term were in order to hear the word of God and worship Him."[56] Carson continues to say that, "Of particular significance for our study of the church as a heavenly and eschatology entity are those instances in the New Testament where *ekklēsia* has a wider reference than either a local congregation or a house-church."[57]

THE CHURCH'S INCEPTION FROM THE TRIUNE-GODHEAD

The church has existed in the Triune God and was manifested in the Old Testament and then fulfilled in Christ's incarnation and sealed by the Holy Spirit at the Day of Pentecost. The Church continues for eternity with Christ as the King, as Carson points out:

---

[55] William M. Ramsay and John H. Leith, *The Church a Believing Fellowship* (Richmond: Covenant Life Curriculum Press, 1965), 69.
[56] D. A. Carson *The Church in the Bible and the World* (Grand Rapids: Baker Book House, 1987), 92.
[57] Ibid., 93.

> To sum up: Heb. 12:23 contains a remarkable reference to *ekklēsia* within the unusual expression, 'the assembly of the first-born'. Verses 22-24 paint the picture of the ultimate, eschatological encounter with God (Rev. 4:5). He, as the judge of all, and Jesus, the mediator of a new covenant, are at the center of that vast assembly, comprising myriad of angels and believers of all ages, i.e. those perfected by the work of Christ, in other words, the whole company of heaven…. The letter of Hebrews reflects the already-not yet found elsewhere in the New Testament, and this point to the fact that Christians live in the overlap of the two ages.[58]

The church of Christ is the assembly of His people and exists and lives in Christ and will continue to live and exist in Christ for eternity. The church resembles the Triune God in fellowship with Himself in three persons. Peter Toon James Spiceland write: "There is one God and only one. This God exists eternally in three distinct persons: the Father, the Son and the Holy Spirit. These three are fully equal in every divine essence. They possess alike the fullness of the divine essence."[59] The concept is not that God is one in the same respect in which He is three Gods but that there is unity of essence and that this essence is shared alike by each of the three persons. The three are conjoined in the total harmony of the will and being far beyond imagination, surpassing the unity observed in humanity. Carson observes that, "The history of God with the world is not, however, to be thought of as no more than a manifestation of what God is already in Himself in eternity. God really opens Himself for the experience of history…. For this reason, the Trinitarian history of God is not sufficiently described by the inference to the Trinity in the origin."[60]

The church does not begin with men but originated from eternity. The Godhead had the original plan for the church before creation.

---

[58] Ibid., 97.

[59] Peter Toon and James D. Spiceland, *One God in Trinity* (London: Samuel Bagster Publishers, 1980), 1.

[60] Ibid., 127

Toon and Spiceland notes that when the Godhead spoke "let us make man in Gen.1:26, "Let us make *na'seh* suggests and confirm Trinity." If Christ is the bridge groom and the head of the church existed before the creation, it is logically true to conclude that the church's inception was in the Trinity. Christ as human, confirmed in Gospel of Matthew 28:18-20 that, "All power is given unto me in heaven and in earth. Go ye therefore, and teach all nations, baptizing them in the name of the Father, and the Son, and of the Holy Spirit."

The doctrine of the Holy Trinity is confirmed by the scriptures.

> The scripture doctrine of the Holy Trinity, as it is asserted in the Westminster confession of faith and catechisms, may be reduced to the following articles of Christian faith; viz. 1. That there is but one and only living and true God. 2. That there are three distinct persons in that one ever-blessed Godhead. 3. That the first person of the Godhead is the Son Jesus Christ. 4. That the Son of God is the same in substance, equal in power and glory with the Father. 5. That the Holy Ghost is the true God co-equal and co-essential with the Father and the Son.[61]

The church finds its inception and origin from the Godhead who manifests grace, love, and fellowship. Paul knew and understood it fully and in his Epistle to the Corinthians, he sums it up, "May the grace of the Lord Jesus Christ, and the love of God, and the fellowship of the Holy Spirit be with you all" (2 Cor. 13:14). This is one of the most important Trinitarian statements of the Christian faith. *Koinonia*, translated as fellowship and communion, implies having things in common and partaking with each other. This text and Matthew 3:16-17 as well as Matthew 28:19 affirm the doctrine of Holy Trinity. Brian Edgar observes, "In these three majestic, grace-filled, divine movements, Paul outlines all that God has done in bringing salvation to the world: God acted to bring all things in heaven and on earth together under one head,

---

[61]   Charles Mastertown, *The Doctrine of the Holy Trinity* (Edinburgh: Andrew Elliot, 1880), 45.

even Christ. God's plan has individual, communal and even cosmic dimensions."[62] The fact that Christ existed in eternity proves that the church's inception was in the Trinity because Christ is the bridegroom and that became real and visible after creation.

The assurance of the Trinity is beautifully summed up by Edward Bickersteth who states, "The scripture assures us of one true knowledge of one God in three personalities; God the Father, God the Son, and God the Holy."[63] This supreme mystery must transcend all human powers and thoughts. Without the Trinity, the church would not exist. The Triune relationships of the Father, Son, and Holy Spirit prepared and planned for the salvation of man. Bruce Ware writes:

> The three persons are never in conflict of purpose, never jealous over another's position or specific work, never prideful over one's own position or work, and they are always sharing fully the delight in being the one God and accomplishing the unified purpose of God. Here is a unity of differentiation, where love abounds and where neither jealousy nor pride is known. Each divine Person accepts his role, each in proper relation to the others and each works together with the others for unified, common purpose.[64]

The three Persons of the Godhead exhibit distinct relationships with each other. They have distinct tasks and activities fulfilling the common plan and they do all this in harmony and in unity. Bruce propounds that, "As we understand better the nature of Trinity the unity and diversity in the ways God had revealed himself to us we have the opportunity to pattern what we do after God's design. We are made in the image of God, and so we can live rightly and best only when we mirror ourselves

---

[62]   Brian Edgar, *The Message of the Trinity* (Downers Grove: InterVarsity Press, 2004), 54.

[63]   Edward Henry Bickersteth, *The Trinity* (Grand Rapids: Kregel Publications, 1984), 144.

[64]   Bruce A. Ware, *Father, Son, and Holy Spirit* (Wheaton: Good News Publishers, 2005), 20.

in relationship to God the eternal Father."[65] The doctrine of Trinity affirms that God's whole undivided essence fully belongs to the distinct Persons of the Godhead eternally, equally, and simultaneously. There is no division whatsoever. The members of the Godhead each possess the divine nature equally. When the earth was created, including man, God did not plan for the salvation of man after the "accident" of man's fall. The Godhead had preplanned the salvation of mankind because He is omniscient, omnipotent and omnipresent. God is not man who is taken by surprise, but He knew what would happen to man and orchestrated a salvation plan through Christ Jesus.

John Calvin's concept of the Trinity relates to the Eastern and the Western approaches. Robert Letham writes: "His focus on the three persons rather than the one essence is more like the Eastern approach than the Western. In much of what he writes, Calvin combines elements of both East and West…. He insists that God is not truly known unless He is distinctly conceived as Triune, and that the fruit of baptism is that God the Father adopts us in his Son and through the Spirit re-forms us into righteousness."[66]

Calvin argued strongly that the Son was *autotheos,* i.e., the Son is God Himself. Calvin was driven to assert that strongly because Valentine Gentile insisted that the Father alone is *autotheos,* contending that God the Father alone is uncreated and has divine essence. Gentile thought that the Son and the Spirit are of a different essence produced by the Father.

The church finds her inception and the roots of her existence in the Godhead. Timothy George states: "Christian initiation brings us, first of all, into a personal family relationship with God the Father, the creator of heaven and earth, who instituted the saving plan to redeem the world through his Son. We receive the courage to call upon him as our Father and to see ourselves as his sons and daughters."[67] The church is truly the body of Christ. Christians are the members of the body of Christ through interpersonal communion *communio personarum.*

---

[65]   Ibid., 22.

[66]   Robert Letham, *The Holy Trinity* (Phillipsburg: P & R Publishing, 2004), 254.

[67]   Timothy George, *God the Holy Trinity* (Grand Rapids: Baker Academic, 2006), 26.

ELECTION

The Epistle to the Ephesians chapter one captures well the whole concept of predestination, election, redemption, and salvation before the foundation of the earth. God foreknew the predicament that man would be in and then preplanned for the salvation of His children. The fundamental doctrines of election and predestination are found in Christ who is the foundation and the finisher of our faith. John Calvin propounds that,

> The foundation and first cause, both our calling and of all the benefits which we receive from God, is here declared to be his eternal election….He hath chosen us before the foundation of the world. The very time when the election took place proves it to be free, for what merit did we possess before the world was made? Chosen in Christ is the second proof that the election is free; it is not of ourselves.[68]

Calvin highlights that the choice is solely from God and that the main focus of that choice depends on and is in Christ. He states that nothing comes from men because Christ's election was before creation. He says that this is the true fountain from which we must draw our knowledge of divine mercy. God has predestined His elect to inherit the kingdom of God, not because they deserve it by merit, but because of love, mercy, and grace from Him.

Calvin puts it so beautifully when he states that,

> In adopting us, therefore, God does not inquire what we are, and is not reconciled to us by any personal worth. His single motive is the eternal good pleasure, by which he predestined us….This intimates, that, in the freest manner, and on no mercenary grounds, does God bestow upon us his love and favor, just as, when we were

---

[68] John Calvin, *Commentaries on the Epistles of Paul to the Galatians and Ephesians* (Grand Rapids: Baker Book House, 1996), 196.

not yet born, and when he was prompted by nothing but his own will, he fixed upon us his choice. The material causes both of eternal election, and the love which is now revealed, is Christ, beloved. This name is given, to remind us that by him the love of God is communicated to us.[69]

Paul highlights three fundamental truths in Ephesians 1:4. He proves that election was before the foundation of the world, the choice was done in Christ, and that election was bestowed only on those whom God chose through His act of love mercy, and grace. Paul also points out that Christ is the source and the foundation of our redemption. By His death, he restored us to God the Father. This was all done according to the riches of His grace and in all wisdom. It is a great mystery. According to Colyar,

Musterion, according to New Testament is not a thing unknowable but it is that which is hidden, a secret kept in the divine counsel, and which would remain such but for Divine revelation.... Believers are blessed in that they were chosen of God before the foundation of the world. It was an act of sovereign grace antecedent to all time. That act was not predicted upon man's choice of God, for man in his deep depravity is devoid of right choices.... God chose them in Christ. In Christ, they are new creatures: old things have passed, all things are become new.[70]

These assertions lead to a simple syllogism: If God elected His people before the foundation of the world in Christ, it means that before the foundation of the world (i.e. before creation), He sets apart the *ekklēsia*, which existed before creation: not in a visible sense but invisible, meaning that the church was conceived before creation in the

---

[69] Ibid., 201.

[70] Nelson R. Colyar, *Expository Notes on the Book of Ephesians* (Little Rock: Challenge Press, 1972), 11.

mind of God. Therefore, the church was in Christ before creation took place.

Nelson Colyar writes: "Believers are blessed in that the high purpose of God in their election is, in its ultimate consummation, that they should appear before Him 'holy and without blame'. Believers are blessed in that God in love foreordained them unto adoption of sons through Jesus Christ unto Himself. He designed it, before ever man was made or even the foundation of the earth was laid, that every believer in Christ Jesus should be placed in position of a son unto Himself."[71]

H.A. Ironside affirms that God predestined believers to be holy and blameless before Him. He expounds the concept that Christians are elected by God to appear before Him holy and without spot for His good pleasure:

> In love, he predestined us unto the adoption of children by Jesus Christ to Himself, according to the pleasure of His will (Eph. 1:4, 5). This is the gist of the doctrine of election. This is the beauty of the salvation story. It is God Himself who purposed our salvation in eternity. It is Jesus Christ who wrought out our salvation upon the cross when the fullness of time had come. It is God the Holy Spirit who convicts us and brings us to repentance and to the knowledge of the grace of God as revealed in Christ. We cannot take any credit to ourselves for our salvation. According as He hath chosen us in Him before the foundation of the world, it pleased Him to do so.[72]

Charles Spurgeon said that in God certainly must have chosen him before he came into this world or He never would have done so afterwards. He sets His love upon us from eternity past. This is a mystery that cannot be understood fully without the insight of the Holy Spirit.

Many theological scholars struggle with the question of how God

---

[71] Ibid., 19.

[72] H. A. Ironside, *In the Heavenlies: Practical Expository Addresess on the Epistle to the Ephesians* (Neptune, New Jersey: Loizeaux Brothers, 1979), 25.

could choose His elect before the foundation of the world and before they were created. Ironside answers it this way: "God who is infinite in wisdom, with whom the past and the future are all one eternal now, purposed in His heart before the world came into existence, that he was going to have people who would be to the praise and glory of His grace for eternity, and He looked down through the ages and saw us as those for whom He would give His Son in order to add to the glory of the Lord Jesus Christ."[73] If Christ chose and elected His own before creation, it inevitably follows that the church was conceived before creation. Ironside concludes: "It is God who purposes it this way, it is God who plans, and it is God who chose us in Christ before the foundation of the world... it is not that He chose the church as such, but He chose every individual who was to be a member of the church, to be one with Christ for eternity."[74] Before the creation of this world, God chose us in Christ so that we would be with Christ for all eternity.

Election is based on God's will and is according to His grace. The words used in this passage are very fundamental: chose; predestined; good pleasure; will; 'purposed'; 'appointed'; 'plan; they all indicate God's sovereign purpose in choosing out a people for Himself. This idea is reminiscent of Old Testament times when God chose the nation of Israel to fulfill His sovereign purpose. Andrew Lincoln propounds:

> God's choice of his people in Christ is said to have taken place 'before the foundation of the world.' This phrase indicates an element in the thinking about election which cannot be found in the election and occurs only later in the Jewish literature.... Elsewhere in the NT the phrase 'before the foundation of the world' is used of God's love for Christ (John 17:24) and his purpose for Christ (I Pet. 1:20), but in regard to believers passages elsewhere in the Pauline corpus provide the closest parallels. In 2 Thess. 2:13 the best reading is probably as a reference to God's choice from the beginning of time. In 2 Tim. 1:9 grace is said to have been given to

---

[73] Ibid. 26
[74] Ibid., 30.

believers before eternal times, while in Rom. 8:29 the prefix in προγνώσκεω "to foreknow," is usually held to indicate that God's electing knowledge of believers precedes not simply their knowledge of him but the creation of the world.[75]

If God's election of all the believers took place before the foundation of the world in Christ, this presupposes the existence of Christ before the foundation of the world (Col. 1:15, 16). The choice of the church precedes the foundation of the world. As Lincoln writes: "So if there is be any talk of the preexistence of the church, it can only be of 'ideal' preexistence, i.e., in the mind or counsel of God."[76] The Trinity planned the salvation of the elect before time and executed the plan through after creation and fulfilled it in the incarnation of Christ. Therefore Cornelius Vanderwaal rightly concludes: "The sanctification of the church, the forgiveness of its sins through Christ, the seal of the Holy Spirit as a guarantee of the coming inheritance all this is possible only through God's election in Christ."[77]

It is a mystery to understand how God chose believers before the foundation of the world. However, since God is omniscient, omnipresent, and omnipotent, we understand why we cannot understand how God elects His own people nor can we comprehend God's sovereign grace. Spence and Exell contend that, "Literally, he chose us out, or selected us for himself (middle voice). The Father chose the heirs of salvation, selected those who were to be quickened from the dead and saved. He chose them in Christ in connection with his work and office as Mediator, giving them to him to be redeemed, not after man was created, nor after man had fallen, but before the foundation of the world."[78] This is the design of God's electing act. The verb "chose" (*exelexato*) is the common

[75] Andrew T. Lincoln, *Word Biblical Commentary: Ephesians* (Nashville: Thomas Nelson, 1990), 23.
[76] Ibid., 24.
[77] Cornelius Vanderwaal, *Search the Scripture*, vol. 9 (St. Catherines: Paideia Press, 1979), 59.
[78] H. D. M. Spence and Joseph S. Exell, *The Pulpit Commentary*, vol. 20 (Grand Rapids: Wm. B. Eerdmans, 1962), 2.

one employed in the LXX in connection with God's choice for Israel. It implies to take a smaller number out of a larger number. The church is the called-out assembly of those who were and are adopted in Christ. This is love that will never end.

Frank and Douglas state: "The ultimate aim throughout the divine plan of redemption is that the recognition of God's merciful dealings with men, which are his glory, should evoke unlimited praise. Redemption has to do with emancipation either of slaves or of prisoners."[79] The main reason God has chosen the elect is for them to be holy and without blame before Him. Election in Christ precedes being blessed with all the spiritual blessings because we are only in Him when we are chosen in Him. Philpot summarizes this when he asserts:

> Jesus Christ, therefore, is the Head of election and of the elect of God; for as in the natural body the head was not first formed and then members, but head and members were by one and the same act called at the same moment into being; so it was with Christ mystical. God the Father did not choose Christ first to be a Mediator, and then choose his people by a subsequent act, and put them into him, which would be setting up a Head without members, a Bridegroom without a bride, a Shepherd without sheep, and a Vine without branches; but chose him and them in him by one eternal act…. Christ was not chosen to be the Son of God by the act of election, for this he ever was and is by virtue of his eternal subsistence; but being already eternal, the Son of the Father in truth and love, and fore-viewed and predestined as incarnate, he was chosen as God-man Mediator, and his people chosen in him as such.[80]

God had a sovereign and divine plan to save a significant portion

---

[79] Frank E. Gaebelein and J. D. Douglas, *The Expository Bible Commentary*, vol. 11 (Grand Rapids: Zondervan, 1978), 24.

[80] J. C. Philpot, *Meditations on the First Chapter of the Epistle to the Ephesians* (Hapenden,U.K.: Gospel Standard Strict Baptist Trust, 1978), 27.

of the human race. The matter of individuals being chosen before the foundation of the world by the predestinating love of God is always understood to be in Christ. R. C. Sproul contends that, "God chose his people in Christ, before the creation of the world, to be holy and blameless in his sight: that is, he set them apart to be a consecrated people, known as saints. It was God's good pleasure not only to prepare the kingdom for the Son, the heirs of God and joint-heirs with Christ. Election is in Christ, leading to adoption into the family of God."[81] God does the electing according to His will and pleasure. It is His sovereign and divine plan, hence His goal of predestination.

PREDESTINATION

Predestination is an act of God in eternity. The Greek verb can equally be translated "predestinate" or "predetermine." Predestination means that God chose the elect to be conformed to the image of his Son. In Ephesians 1:5, Paul uses the Greek verb, having "predestined" us that we should be holy and without blame before Him. Predestination is a manifestation of the love of the Father. He predestined us to the adoption of children. In 1Corinthians 2:7, the verb "predetermine" is used: "But we speak the wisdom of God in a mystery, even the hidden wisdom, which God ordained before the world unto our glory." Gordon Clark states, "Greek grammar allows the participle *'having predestined us'* to be pictured as contemporaneous with the calling. In the Septuagint this Hebrew word is *ratson*. God's good pleasure is translated, not only by *eudokia,* the word for 'good pleasure' found in Ephesians, but also by other words meaning 'will,' 'an act of will,' and the verb 'to will.' "[82]

The church's inception before creation is clearly seen in these biblical passages. Predestination was planned before creation and it was initiated after creation. Frank Gaebelein writes: "It has to do with those who through Christ are to be received into God's family by adoption. Under

---

[81] R.C. Sproul, *The Purpose of God: Ephesians* (Ross-Shire: Christian Focus Publications, 2006), 24.
[82] Gordon H. Clark, *Predestination* (Phillipsburg: Presbyterian and Reformed Publishing Company, 1969), 71.

Roman law, an adopted son enjoyed the same status and privileges as a real son. Christ is God's Son 'by nature.' Believers are so only by adoption and grace, yet they are co-heirs with him (Rom. 8:17). The ground of this gracious action is to be discovered in the character of God himself. Behind the fulfillment of his perfect will there lies his pleasure *eudokia* that which brings satisfaction because it represents the expression of his being."[83]

Are there any differences between election and predestination as they are being used by Paul? There are some differences although they are almost identical. Philpot defines them to some extent:

> Election is the first act in the mind of God whereby he chose the persons of the elect to be holy and without blame, and that predestination was the second act, which ratified by fixed decree the state of those to whom election had given birth. Having chosen them in his dear Son unto a perfection of holiness and righteousness, his love went forth, not only to fix their state by firm decree, but to add another blessing, the highest and greatest which even his love could bestow: to make them His own children by adoption, and thus himself become their Father and their God.[84]

On the same note, Matthew Henry points out:

> Election, or choice, respects that lump or mass of mankind out of which some are chosen, from which they are separated and distinguished. Predestination has respect to the blessings they are designed for; particularly the adoption of the children, it being the purpose of God that in due time we should become his adopted children, and so have a right to all the privileges and to the inheritance of children. We have the date of

[83] Frank E. Gaebelein, *The Expositors' Bible Commentary*, vol. 2 (Grand Rapids: Zondervan Publishing House, 1978), 24.

[84] Philpot, *Meditations*, 34.

this act of love: it was before the foundation of the world; not only before God's people had a being, but before the world had a beginning; for they were chosen in the counsel of God from all eternity.[85]

All who are chosen to happiness as the end are chosen to holiness as the means. John Calvin states that, "We are predestined by adoption to himself through Jesus Christ, according to the good pleasure of his will. When he says that God had predestined us by adoption, it is to show that if we be God's children it is not through nature but though his pure grace. Now this pure grace is not in respect of anything that God foresaw in us but because he had marked us out before hand and appointed us to such adoption, yes, even in such a way that the cause of it is not to be sought elsewhere than in himself."[86]

The apostle Peter states the same concept as the apostle Paul. First Peter 1:2 says "Elect according to the foreknowledge of God the Father, through sanctification of the Spirit, unto obedience and sprinkling of the blood of Jesus Christ: grace unto you, and peace, be multiplied." The *eklektosis,* "elect," are the chosen people of God and brought to faith in Christ. Edmond asserts that, "The verbal adjective 'elect' is passive, marking the readers as the objects of the electing action of God, who is the unnamed agent. They were chosen by God to be His own in order that they might be partakers of the heavenly inheritance being reserved for them (1:4)."[87] Peter made it clear that their election served God's purpose. Election involves responsibility and accountability. Peter was sending the words of comfort and assurance to Christians who were in the Diaspora: "Elect according to the foreknowledge of God the Father, through sanctification of the Spirit, unto obedience and sprinkling of the blood of Jesus Christ." Sinners are chosen by the foreknowledge of God the Father. The election is God's knowledge and plan, i.e. He predestined us in Christ. John Lillie writes: "The first rule is the

---

[85] Matthew Henry, *Matthew Henry Commentary*, vol. 6 (Mclean: Macdonald Publishing Company, n. d.), 687.

[86] John Calvin, *Sermons on the Epistle to the Ephesians* (Edinburgh: Banner of Truth Trust, 1973), 39.

[87] Hiebert D. Edmond, *1 Peter* (Chicago: Moody Press, 1992), 46.

divine foreknowledge…the scheme of redemption in all its parts being ever in Scripture represented as flowing from the Fountain of Deity. Observe, then, that the election of our text is not according to previous differences of character and moral susceptibility in the objects of it, nor according to their actual faith and repentance, nor yet according to God's foreknowledge of these things in them."[88]

The doctrine of predestination brings into the foreground two Old Testament quotations: Malachi 1:2-3, "Jacob I loved, but Esau I hated," and Exodus 9:16, "I raised you up, Pharaoh, up for this purpose, that I might display my power in you and that my name might be proclaimed in all the earth." Paul summarizes "Therefore hath he mercy on which he will have mercy, and whom he will hardneth." (Rom.9:18). James Montgomery Boyce contends that, "Those two statements concerning election and probation teach that in some respects they are the same: both flow from the eternal counsels or will of God, rather than the will of man, and both are for the end of making the glory of God known. In that respect we can speak of equal ultimacy."[89] In his sermon "Ten Happy Truths About Election" on I Peter 1:1-12 and Romans 2 Joel Beeke asserts:

> The Church is chosen to everlasting life. (1) Sinners are chosen by the Father's foreknowledge. Peter says we are elected so that we may believe. God's knowledge is like a husband's love for his wife. God intimately knows His people with intimate love eternity. (2 Sinners are chosen by God's loving sovereign pleasure alone. (3) Sinners being chosen are the real fountain head of all spiritual blessings. (4) Sinners are chosen through the sanctification of the Holy Spirit. (5) (6) Sinners are chosen in Christ unto obedience with the sprinkling of the blood of Jesus Christ. Sinners are personally chosen. God saves His people one by one as they are gathered

---

[88] John Lillie, *Lectures on the First and Second Epistles of Peter* (Minneapolis: Clock and Clock, 1978), 19.

[89] James Montgomery Boyce, *Romans vol. 3 of God and History Romans 9-11* (Grand Rapids: Baker Books, 1993), 1063.

in. (7) Sinners are chosen to be adopted into a larger family of God, the invisible Church. (8) Sinners can be assured of their election. We know by faith that we are the chosen ones. (9) Sinners are chosen irreversibly or unchangeably. God does not repent of what He has done. (10) Sinners are wonderfully impacted and affected personally by grace and peace.[90]

Joel Beeke highlights the importance and fundamental truths about election. He points out the ten positive good things about election refuting some scholars, especially the Arminians, who criticized John Calvin for stressing the doctrines of predestination and election which Paul and Peter nevertheless taught in their epistles.

REDEMPTION AND ADOPTION

The gospel is good news; it is the message of our redemption by the incarnate Son of God who was delivered to death for our offenses and was raised again for our justification. Meckler defines redemption as "deliverance from sin and uncleanness to purity and holiness. It is a 'finished' work of Christ; he died once for all. God has visited and has redeemed His people. Our redemption covers both the work of Christ for us and the work of the Holy Spirit in us. Redemption is a process as well as a fact."[91] Redemption is accomplished and applied by Christ Jesus. It is done through the sheer grace of God. It is the sovereign love of God. As John Murray writes: "The question is not the relation of the death of Christ to the numerous blessings which those who finally perish may partake of this life. However, the importance of this question is its proper place. The question is precisely the reference of the death of Christ when this death is viewed as vicarious death, that is to say,

---

[90] Joel Beeke, *Sermon on CD, 'Ten Happy Truths About Election,'* Grand Rapids: recording@hnrc.org, October 11, 2009.
[91] Nathaniel Meckler, *The Doctrine of our Redemption* (New York: Abingdon-Cokesbury Press, 1948), 18.

as vicarious obedience, as substitutionary sacrifice, and expiation, as effective propitiation, reconciliation, and redemption."[92]

Redemption involves when Christ redeeming His people, and then adopting them into His family. As Paul said, "He gave himself for us in order that he might redeem us from all iniquity and purify to himself a people for his own possession, zealous of good works" (Tit. 2:14). Ferrell Grisworld states, "Redemption is the work of Christ for His people, whom the Father gave Him before the foundation of the world as His inheritance. This work of paying a ransom, redeeming them, or purchasing them as His peculiar is people in His work as High Priest, and Mediator. The price He paid was His own dear blood which was shed for the satisfaction of justice and the divine law of God."[93] From this understanding, we can see that Christ has paid fully the price of redemption for His people. He redeemed them completely and actually applies all the benefits of salvation to all those He redeemed.

Adoption is one of the benefits of the elect. The adoption concept is a Roman law tradition which Paul knew and saw it lived out. Paul ushers in a new dimension to that concept that those who have been predestined and are the elect of God are adopted into God's family by Christ's atonement and the work of the Holy Spirit. Jeanne Stevenson-Mossier writes, "Many adoptees want to seek, find and connect with their birth parents.... This adoption occurs through the person and work of the Second Person of the Trinity who was without sin and primal woundedness. His cry from the cross, 'My God, my God why have you forsaken me?' becomes the point at which an adoptee knows that he/she is understood in their pain of separation."[94] At adoption a child is accepted and given every right to be a son or daughter in that particular family, including privileges, inheritance, rights, and all that a family member is entitled. "The hermeneutic or the 'lens' of adoption allows us to see that adoption closely follows the Reformed doctrine of

---

[92] John Murray, *Redemption Accomplished and Applied* (Grand Rapids: Eerdmans, 1955), 16.

[93] Ferrell Griswold, *Particular Redemption* (Pensacola: Chapel Library Publications, (n. d.), 3.

[94] Jeanne Stevenson-Mossier, *The Spirit of Adoption* (Louisville: Westminster John Knox Press, 2003), 93.

justification, putting us once again into reunion with our birth parent, God. Simultaneous with our adoption, we are reunited with our birth parent, God."[95] The doctrine of adoption of the elect into God's family is a fundamental plan which the Godhead had before the creation of the world. Christ's atonement was the initial plan to bring back or adopt the elect to God's family. Peterson asserts:

> The doctrine of adoption is one of the most precious doctrines we have as children of God. Just to be called children of God is such a wonderful blessing.... Salvation was planned by the Trinity, especially by God the Father, in choosing people for salvation before the creation of the world. Salvation was accomplished by the Trinity, especially by God the Son, in his death and resurrection. Salvation is applied by the Trinity, especially the Holy Spirit, when he brings grace to bear on the lives of human beings. Salvation will be consummated by the Trinity Father, Son and Holy Spirit in the resurrection of the dead for life in the new heavens and new earth.... 'In love (the Father) predestined us to be adopted as his sons through Jesus Christ' (Eph.1:4-5). Here is the source of tremendous comfort: our son ship was planned by the Father before he made the world. He loves us and chose us to include us in his family before time.[96]

Adoption is grounded in God's prior choice of His people. God chose us for adoption. Peterson continues, "The primary way that God the Father assures us of sonship is by promising in Scripture to adopt us, but that is not the only way. Along with the promise of salvation, God gives us his Holy Spirit."[97] The Spirit of adoption guarantees to us in our hearts that we are God's children (Rom. 8:16). The Scripture presents the church as the family of God, the body of Christ, the temple of the Holy Spirit, the new creation, Christ's bride, and God's flock.

---

[95] Ibid., 93.

[96] Robert A Peterson, *Adopted by God* (Phillipsburg: P & R, 2001), 8.

[97] Ibid., 134.

The adoption of children into the family of God is both present and future in the New Testament. Romans 8:23 states that future sonship embodies the adoption of our bodies. In the mind of God, we were adopted well before the creation of the world. It is fundamentally true, therefore, that the church's inception was before creation. Christians are the adopted children of God not because of what they did or what they deserve but through the grace, love, and mercy of God in Jesus Christ. He elected them, predestined them to be the children of God and then adopted them into His family, the holy catholic church.

David Garner writes, "The important subjects to consider are Soteriology, Pauline adoption, Christology and pneumatology in that the outpouring of the Holy Spirit confirms cosmically and applies existentially to the sons of Adam the completed work of the messianic Son. Through union with Christ by faith, the sons of Adam who dwelt under the curse of the Law graciously receive the righteousness of the Son of God, who accomplished in their place what they were unwilling and unable to do."[98] Adoption is the grafting in of the branches which were cut off because of sin. Those are grafted into the family of God and they become permanent adopted children of God. The work is Christ's through the working of the Holy Spirit who brings those whom Christ has chosen before the foundation of the world to hear His word. They are convicted of, repent of and are forgiven of their sins. They are born again, justified, sanctified and will be glorified when they will be taken by Christ to heaven forever. John Gadsby writes, "An adopted slave was always considered as a real member of the family, and his name was registered as such, not only in the family register, but with the other members of the family, in the archives of the city; and the book in which it was so registered was called in Jerusalem the 'Book of Life,' or the 'Book of the Living.' So the names of all the Lord's adopted ones are registered in the Book of Life of the Heavenly Jerusalem; and the beauty of this is it is also the King's family, not a beggar's, into which he is registered; and he is as welcome at the table as the King himself."[99]

---

[98] David B Garner, "Adoption in Christ," *(Ph.D. dissertation,* Westminster Theological Seminary, 2002), 31.

[99] John Gadsby, Slavery, *Adoption and Redemption* (New Ipswich: Pietan Publications, 1994), 34.

The doctrines of election, predestination and adoption are fundamental to the understanding of God's foreknowledge of His chosen people before the foundation of the world. These doctrines reflect the sovereignty of God and His love, mercy, and grace to those that He loves and whom He chooses to save. The grace of God is beyond human understanding, and many biblical scholars have debated about these doctrines. But Paul in Ephesians and Romans and Peter have clearly pointed out that it is God's will and choice to elect some and reject the reprobates. We have to adhere to what the Bible outlines and not to import human knowledge and reasoning to infer and interpret the scriptures according to our own understanding. Let God be God and man be man.

VISIBLE AND INVISIBLE CHURCH

The church that Christ redeemed is both visible and invisible. The argument that has been forwarded by some scholars is this: Are those who were elected and predestined to be the sons and daughters of the living and everlasting Father publicly known in the church or do they grow together with the weeds as Jesus Christ said in Matthew 13:30? Jesus said, "Let both grow together until the harvest: and in time of harvest I will say to the reapers, gather ye together first the tares, and bind them in bundles to burn them: but gather first the wheat to my barn." John Calvin expounded on the subject of the visible and invisible church. His concept of the visible church as the mother of believers provides an insight to Calvin's perception of the church. He contended:

> But because it is now our intention to discuss the visible church, let us learn even from the simple title "mother" how useful, indeed how necessary, it is that we should know her. For there is no other way to enter into life unless this mother conceives us in her womb, gives us birth, nourishes us at her breast, and lastly, unless she keeps us under her care and guidance until, putting off mortal flesh, we become like the angels (Matthew 22:30). Our weakness does not allow us to be dismissed

from her school until we have been pupils all our lives. Furthermore, away from her bosom one cannot hope for any forgiveness of sins or any salvation, as Isaiah (Isaiah 37:32) and Joel (Joel 2:32) testify. Ezekiel agrees with them when he declares that those whom God rejects from heavenly life will not be enrolled among God's people (Ezekiel 13:9).... By these words God's fatherly favor and the especial witness of spiritual life are limited to his flock, so that it is always disastrous to leave the church.[100]

John Calvin points out that the church is our mother and has the responsibility to feed and nourish her children with the right food. The church is the mother who guides, disciplines, and teaches the children the right paths of righteousness, godliness, gentleness, kindness, patience and all the fruits of the Spirit. The children in turn are obligated to listen to their mother, the church, and follow her instructions. Calvin continues to speak about the visible church. He states,

How we are to judge the church visible, which falls within our knowledge, is, I believe, already evident from the above discussion. For we have said that Holy Scripture speaks of the church in two ways. Sometimes by the term "church" it means that which is actually in God's presence, into which no persons are received but those who are children of God by grace of adoption and true members of Christ by sanctification of the Holy Spirit. Then, indeed, the church includes not only the saints presently living on earth, but all the elect from the beginning of the world. Often, however, the name "church" designates the whole multitude of men spread over the earth who profess to worship one God and Christ. By baptism we are initiated into faith in him; by partaking in the Lord's Supper we attest our

---

[100] John Calvin, *Institutes of the Christian Religion* (Philadelphia: Westminster Press, 1960), 1016.

unity in true doctrine and love; in the Word of the Lord we have agreement, and for the preaching of the Word the ministry instituted by Christ is preserved. In this church are mingled many hypocrites who have nothing of Christ but the name and outward appearance. There are very many ambitious, greedy, envious persons, evil speakers, and some of quite unclean life. Such are tolerated for a time either because they cannot be convicted by a competent tribunal or because a vigorous discipline does not always flourish as it ought. Just as we must believe, therefore, that the former church, invisible to us, visible to the eyes of God alone, so we are commanded to revere and keep communion with the latter, which is called "church" in respect to men.[101]

The church of Jesus Christ is visible and invisible. The being of the church is grounded upon the ontological reality of the divine love that flows into it and fills it. Geddes Macgregor writes, "One cannot point to the body of Christ in the same way in which one might conceivably have pointed to the chief instrument of the Passion.... It has a sacramental significance, for it draws attention to the fact that the church is indeed, the total sacrament. Neither can the visible church nor the visible elements of the Eucharist be identified with the Body of Christ *simpliciter*; yet both are static, visible aspects of the dynamic, ontological reality that is the Christian Church."[102] St. Ignatius believed that the union between Christ and the church began when the eternal Logos united itself to flesh, and that this union was consummated through the death and the resurrection of Christ. "Individual faith is a preliminary to 'fleeing to the flesh of Jesus'. Believing, one is then united to Christ in His church, where one may eventually 'ascend' to God."[103]

Christ is the foundation of the church and the church was in Christ from the beginning, embedded in Christ as Eve was embedded in

---

[101] Ibid., 1024.

[102] Geddes Macgregor, *Corpus Christi: the nature of the Church According to the Reformed Tradition* (Philadelphia: The Westminster Press,1958). 169.

[103] Ibid., 173.

Adam. The church belongs to Christ and the believers, the elect, the chosen ones who were in Christ before the foundation of the world. Earl Radmacher states, "There is a sense, however, in which the term *invisible* may very properly be used of the church. The New Testament knows of no Christian who is not a church member; that is, every regenerate person in this age is a member of the church, the body of Christ. As the pastor of the local church, however, looks out over his flock, he is not able to discern by sight those who are truly regenerate. Only God omniscient is able to do that. 'The union of believers with Christ is a mystical union; the Spirit that unites them constitutes an invisible tie; and the blessings of salvation, such as regeneration, genuine conversion, true faith, and spiritual communion with Christ, are all invisible to the natural eye;-and yet these things constitute the real *forma* (ideal character) of the church."[104]

Union with Christ is invisible and the church is composed of people who are born again Christians and also those who are not genuine Christians. They are those who believe that the church is composed of all true believers in Christ. The church, in terms of the true regenerate and born again Christians, is invisible. No one can tell with absolute certainty who is a true Christian although Christ said that His disciples would be known that they were His own by their fruits. Christ only knows His own because He is omnipotent, omniscient, and omnipresent. The visible church refers to the members of the church who assemble on the Lord's Day and celebrate the Lord's Supper in fellowship. The bread and the wine are visible elements which bring the believers together to commemorate the death and the resurrection of our Lord Jesus Christ. Radmacher asserts, "There is no debate among most theologians as to the origin of the church. The idea of the church began in the counsel of God before the foundation of the world. It is, with all components of the plan of God, in a sense, supra historical. God has related Himself to time, however, and the points where this plan is tangent with history constitute the present subject matter for investigation."[105] Some scholars like Hanke contend, "The church is the natural result of individual

---

[104] Earl D. Radmacher, *What the Church is All About* (Chicago: Moody Press, 1972), 192.
[105] Ibid., 196.

religion in several persons who have the opportunity of personal for association. Religion makes the church an unavoidable necessity..... When they come together thus religiously for worship for mutual religious enjoyment, it is impossible to conduct the worship without regularity, order, rules, and so you have a church"[106] This assertion does not point out the fundamental doctrine and definition the church. The church is not merely the natural result of individual religion; she was founded by Christ. Douglas Bannerman declares, "In the history of Abraham we see the church of God visibly set up, built upon the Gospel declared to him, and the covenant made with him and his seed. There have been believing men and preachers of righteousness before Abraham.... But now, for the first time in the record of revelation, we find God by His word and providence distinctly separating to Himself a little company of men who are called and chosen, and faithful."[107]

The fundamental truth of the foundation of the church upon the Rock is Jesus Christ the Lord. As to the actual stage in which Jesus founded the visible church, several suggestions are presented. Johnston categorizes them: "1. The call of the first disciples; 2. The confession of Peter as representative of the Twelve; 3. The last Supper, which established a New Covenant, to be sealed by Christ's death; 4. The union of the disciples in the Resurrection faith, that is, either at Easter itself with the appearances to Peter, the Apostles, or the five hundred brethren; or at the Pentecostal gift of the promised Spirit."[108] Although Johnston's declaration is correct, it only relates to the New Testament when Christ commissioned and fulfilled the prophecies of the Old Testament. It does not relate to the initial founding of the church before creation. The invisible church was founded by the Triune God before the foundation of the world.

Some scholars assert that the church was established by Christ during His time on earth. Richard Clearwaters says, "The Church, therefore, was established in the days of Jesus' sojourn in the flesh and

---

[106] Howard A. Hanke, *From Eden to Eternity* (Grand Rapids: Eerdmans, 1960), 100.

[107] D. Douglas Bannerman, *The Scripture Doctrine of the Church* (Grand Rapids: Eerdmans, 1955), 43.

[108] Johnston George, *The Doctrine of the Church in the New Testament* (Cambridge: University Publications, 1943), 46.

the work of its construction was begun with the material prepared by John the Baptist, later the twelve apostles of our Lord."[109] This statement is correct in regards to the inauguration of the Kingdom of God on earth by the incarnate Christ but not on the basis of the foundation of the church, the inception of the church. The inception was before the foundation of the world. I concur with Charles Baker who said, "Perhaps the most evident distinction...is the fact that the church of Matthew and of Pentecost is one which was prophesied or predicted by the Old Testament prophets, whereas the church of Paul's epistle is specifically declared to be part of a great body of truth which in former ages had been hidden in God and never before revealed to the sons of men (Eph. 3:5, 9; Col. 1:24-26; Ps. 22:22 as quoted in Heb. 2:12) is evidence that there was a church predicted in the Old Testament."[110]

To understand what John Calvin thought about the visible church and his perception, he states,

> When in the Creed we profess to believe the Church, reference is made not only to the visible Church of which we are treating, but also to all the elect of God, including in the number even those who have departed this life.... Judgment which ought to be formed concerning the visible Church which comes under our observation, must, I think, be sufficiently clear from what has been said. I have observed that the Scriptures speak of the Church in two ways. Sometimes when they speak of the Church they mean the Church as it really is before God the Church into which none are admitted but those who by the gift of adoption are sons of God, and by the sanctification of the Spirit true members of Christ. In this case it only comprehends the saints who dwell on the earth, but all the elect who have existed from the beginning of the world.... As it is necessary to believe in

---

[109] Richard V. Clearwaters, *The Local Church of the New Testament* (Chicago: Conservative Baptist Association, 1954), 26.

[110] Charles F. Baker, *Bible Truth: What We Believe and Why We Believe it* (Milwaukee: Milwaukee Bible College, 1956), 69.

the invisible Church, which is manifest to the eye of God only, so we are also enjoined to regard this Church which is so called with reference to man, and to cultivate its communion.... We have said that the symbols by which the Church is discerned are the preaching of the word and the observance of the sacraments, for these cannot anywhere exist without producing fruit and prospering by the blessings of God.[111]

The church, which is the called-out assembly is an established spiritual kingdom that includes believers from all nations from every language, tribe, and creed. Stanford Murrell writes, "the whole visible body of professing Christians throughout the world is called the Church. (I Cor. 15:9; Gal. 1:13; Matt.16:18). It is called visible because its members are known and its assemblies are public. God called His people to organize themselves into distinct visible communities, with constitutions and rules, for the great purpose of giving visibility to the kingdom, of making known the Gospel of that kingdom, and of gathering in its chosen subjects."[112]

The visible church has been mandated by Christ to preach the Gospel to all the nations. Although no one can infallibly discern the true believer, God has allowed believers to work together in His church and carry on the activities of the church. The activities of the church are done through the work of the Holy Spirit who works in the lives of believers, uniting them for one purpose.

Murrell continues, "*ekklesia* also denotes the invisible church, the whole body of the redeemed, all those whom the Father has given to Christ (Eph. 55:23-29; Heb. 12:23). The invisible church is a pure society, the church in which Christ dwells, the body of Christ. It is called invisible because the greater parts of those who constitute it are already in heaven or are yet unborn, and also because its members are still on

---

[111] John Calvin, *Calvin's Institutes* (Grand Rapids: Associated Publishers And Authors, 1564), 544.
[112] Stanford E. Murrell, *Glorious Institution: The Church in History* (Pensacola: Mount Zion Publications, 1998), 12.

earth and cannot be distinguished with certainty.... It is unseen except by Him who searches the heart."[113]

The church is the mystery of the body of Christ. She will be fully realized when the Bridegroom comes to take His bride to be with Him forever. The church is both visible and invisible. It is visible in the sense that the membership is visible and participates in the body of Christ in baptism and the celebration of the Lord's Supper. It is invisible in the sense that no one knows whom Christ has chosen. We are all limited in knowing the hearts of people but the Bible is very clear that anyone who believes and repents from his/her sins will be forgiven and be saved (Acts 2:21).

CONCLUSION

The church originated in the mind of and decree of God before the creation of world. The Triune Godhead Sovereignly planned for the redemption of His chosen people. Paul spoke about those who were elected before the foundation of the world in Ephesians 1:1-14 and Romans 8:17, and Peter also alluded to the elect of God being chosen before the foundation of the world (1 Peter 1:2). Predestination is clearly indicated in the portions of scriptures which state that this is the work of Christ through the love of God and sanctification of the Holy Spirit. God's foreknowledge in predestination is for the good of His chosen people. The elect are redeemed from their sins through repentance, forgiveness of sins, and are justified and are sanctified by the Holy Spirit. After redemption, they are adopted into the family of God.

The family of God is the church, the bride of Christ. She is both the visible and the invisible church. The church is visible because of her membership and in the participation in the sacraments. It is invisible because it is the mystery of the body of Christ. No one knows the true chosen people of God because it is God alone who knows and searches the hearts of the people. The unity of the church brings the children of God together to worship Him in truth and in spirit.

---

[113] Ibid., 13.

CHAPTER 4

THE CHURCH'S
INCEPTION
THEOLOGICALLY

THE THREEFOLD OFFICE OF CHRIST

In Old Testament times, Yahweh chose certain individuals and anointed them to serve Him in the offices of prophet, priest and king. James Beeke writes, "Old Testament prophets, priests, and kings were pointed to, and pictured, the work of Christ. Only Jesus Christ, however, was appointed to serve in all three offices. Only Jesus Christ could perform and fulfill all of God's required demands to be a perfect and divine Prophet, Priest, and King."[114] There have been some controversies about Christ holding three offices in His incarnation, especially in liberal schools of thought. However, the evangelical view has proved that the incarnate Christ held the three positions, as this chapter will show.

Christ Jesus was ordained to these offices from eternity. James Beeke writes: "Old Testament prophecy testifies of Him as the great Prophet, Priest, and King who would come. The New Testament confirms that He is the great office-bearer the Word (Prophet), the Lamb (Priest), and the Lord of Lords (King)."[115] The three sorts of persons who used

---

[114] James W. Beeke, *Bible Doctrine for Teens and Young Adults* (Grand Rapids: WM. B. Eerdmans, 1988), 11.
[115] Ibid., 11.

to be anointed under the law-prophets (I Kings 19:16), priests, (Exo. 27:7), and kings-all served as types that pointed to Christ. These three offices met in Christ who was anointed for the execution of them all (Isaiah 61:1). Christ was anointed to preach the good tidings unto the meek, as a prophet; to bind up the brokenhearted as a Priest; and to proclaim liberty as a King. He was not anointed with earthly oil, as the former prophets, the priests, and the kings under the Old Testament dispensation, but with the oil of the Spirit. Each office will be discussed and explained, separately, starting with Christ's office as a prophet. This entire plan was laid before the foundation of the world for the sake of His chosen people. As the Head of the church, Christ had to undertake all three offices, in order to redeem the bride, His church. Christ as the Head of the church is inseparable from His church.

CHRIST AS PROPHET

"The LORD thy God will raise up unto thee a prophet from the midst of thee, of thy brethren, like unto me; unto him ye shall hearken" (Deut.18:15). In the Old Testament, a prophet was ordained and qualified to speak for God unto men. First, he received God's word, then he brought and taught the Word of God to the people. The first person the Bible calls a prophet (in Hebrew, *nabi*) was Abraham (Gen.20:7). But Old Testament prophecy received its normative form in the life and person of Moses who constituted a standard of comparison for all future prophets. A. Douglas says, "Every feature which characterized the true prophet of Yahweh in the classical tradition of Old Testament prophecy was first found in Moses. He received a specific call from God. The initiative in making a prophet rests with God."[116]

When Christ made Himself known as a teacher and a prophet sent by God, He took upon Himself the office of purifying the temple in order to arouse the Jews to make them more attentive. J. M. Jansen writes, "The first narrative is given by John only in the second chapter of his Gospel. But now, towards the end of his course, claiming again for himself the same power, he warns the Jews of the pollutions of the

---

[116] Douglas, *The New Bible Dictionary*, 1036.

temple, and at the same time points out that a new restoration is at hand. Yet, there is no reason to doubt that he declared himself to be both King and High Priest, who presided over the temple and the worship of God." [117]

The Hebrew word *nava* actually means to experience heat from within and the zeal to be sent out. The Word of God boils in one's spirit and then it sends one to the people with a message from God, like Jeremiah. Christ as the prophet had a burning desire to do the will of God. A prophet in the Old Testament had authority from Yahweh to speak the Word of God without error. Jesus Christ as prophet had that authority and the people marveled at Him when he demonstrated that He had authority and power. Christ spoke as a representative of the Triune God. Christ was the incarnate prophet who was in the beginning and the world was created by him, (John 1:1). Believers were in Christ in God's decree before the creation of the world.

The prophetical office of Christ is confirmed by both prophecy and fulfillment. Brakel writes: "He was promised as a prophet in Deuteronomy 18:15, Acts 3:22, confirms that this reference is to Christ; these very words are quoted as relating to Christ. In his sojourn upon earth the Lord presented himself as a prophet."[118] The Lord Jesus conducted himself as a prophet. He was recognized as such by the people. "A great prophet is risen up among us....which was a prophet mighty in deed and word before God and all the people" (Luke 24:19). Brakel concludes: "The ministry of the prophets consisted in 1) reception of immediate revelation from God concerning divine mysteries which occurred among prophets with an extraordinary calling; 2) the proclamation and exposition of the word of God; 3) the foretelling of the future events; 4) confirmation of revelation by means of miracles."[119] To confirm that Christ was a prophet: first the prophets received divine mysteries and revelation (Num. 12: 6), so Christ Jesus received all these things from God, His Father in that fashion. Secondly, the ministry of the prophets consisted of exposition and proclamation of the Word of God; the Lord

---

[117] John Frederick Jansen, *Calvin's Doctrine of the Work of Christ* (London: James Clark, 1956), 39.

[118] a 'Brakel, *Christian's* 1. 519.

[119] Ibid., 519.

Jesus did expounded the word and fulfilled it. Thirdly, the prophetic office consisted of foretelling future events. Christ predicted what He would encounter in order to merit salvation for His elect, but also what would church and the world would go through on the Day of Judgment. Fourthly, just as the prophets demonstrated and confirmed their offices by means of miracles, Jesus confirmed the authenticity of his prophetic office by performing miracles (John 7:31). The prophets performed miracles by the power of Jesus Christ. Brakel notes: "Just as Christ conducted himself in respect to the law, so likewise he proclaimed the gospel as a prophet."[120]

Brakel asserts that Christ administered His prophetical office by His prophets in the Old Testament during his sojourn upon earth (Heb.1:1-2), and even after the ascension, He continued to administer His prophetical office by means of His apostles, teachers and pastors (Eph. 4:11). There is a twofold administration of His prophetic office, external and internal. "Christ administers His prophetical office externally by the written and printed Word, and by the Word preached by His servants. Christ administered His prophetic office internally when by His Spirit He illuminates souls by His marvelous light (I Pet. 2:9). He illuminates the heart to give the light of the knowledge of the glory of God in the face of Jesus Christ (2 Co. 4:6), enabling them to understand the truth in its essence (Eph. 4:21), and to have the mind of Christ (I Cor. 2:16)."[121] As a prophet, Christ teaches with authority. He is all-knowing, almighty, and perfect.

Martin Luther, the great reformer, struggled many years under deep convictions of sin and guilt. As a monk and professor of theology, he studied the writings of many church fathers and the Bible. His mind was continually occupied with religious teachings. However, approximately 1512, as he was studying for his lecture series on the Book of Romans, he read Romans 1:17, the last part, "the just shall live by faith." The Holy Spirit enlightened his understanding and this truth of scripture penetrated his heart. Christ, as teaching prophet, spoke to him, showing him that salvation is by faith in the righteousness of Christ, and not in man's merits. The Spirit revealed Christ to Luther. His heart melted. Joy

---

[120]   Ibid., 521.
[121]   Ibid., 522.

replaced sadness, light dispelled darkness, and peace filled his restless soul.[122]

As a prophet, teaching by his Word and Spirit, Christ performed in the life of Luther that which no human teachers can accomplish.

A prophet spoke with authority from God and people listened to the message. Even the Pharisees marveled at Christ's preaching because he preached with power and authority. Christ spoke on behalf of the Trinity but He was God incarnate. He spoke the truth and He was Truth. The Lord has also made known in His Word what the church of the New Testament would encounter until the end of the world. In one of his lectures, Joel Beeke said, "We need Christ as a prophet, for we are not able to discover the mind and will of God on our own. We need to remember that in the history of redemption, revelation always precedes redemption. Experientially, Jesus as a prophet uncovers our misery by showing us both who God is and who we are. He reveals Himself to be desirable and necessary and precious, too. He teaches us continually so as to work sanctification in our lives."[123]

Christ in his office of prophet was a teacher of doctrine during his earthly ministry. Calvin remarks "The prophets pointed to the great messianic teacher who was to come. They hoped for the full light of understanding only at the coming of the Messiah. Christ as a teacher of the Word of God bears the perfection of the gospel doctrine. God revealed Himself to the Old Testament people Israel; yet this revelation was in the shadows, in partial form through the prophets."[124] God continues to speak by the Holy Spirit through His written word. Christ as prophet continues to teach by the Spirit. He is the representative of Godhead for the redemption of His church as prophet.

CHRIST AS PRIEST

"The Lord hath sworn, and will not repent, Thou art a priest forever after the order of Melchizedek" (Psalm 110:4). Christ's work as High

---

[122] Beeke, *Bible Doctrine*, 19.

[123] Joel R. Beeke, *"Christology,"* March 19, 2008.

[124] Peterson, *Calvin and the Atonement*, 48.

Priest accomplished the atonement of the elect. The priest (*coheen*), is one who is taken among men ordained for men in things pertaining to God, that he may offer both gifts and sacrifices for sins (Heb.5:1). James Beeke asserts that, "In the Old Testament, a priest performed three important duties;

a. Sacrifices (or offering) pictured by the priest's offering an animal upon the brazen alter of burnt offerings.
b. Praying (or interceding) portrayed by the priest's offering incense upon the golden alter of incense.
c. Blessing displayed by the priest's returning to bless the people after performing his work."[125]

The Old Testaments prophets predicted that Christ would come as a great High Priest to do His priestly work. The New Testament has confirmed the fulfillment of the prophecies. The Lord Jesus performs the work of sacrificing, praying, and blessing for the elect. He did that work at the cross and He is still doing it for those who come to Him. As James Beeke puts it, "The primary work of a prophet was to serve as God's representative to men to present God before the people. The primary work of a priest was to be man's representative before God to present man before God."[126]

John Calvin confirms the priesthood of Christ by remarking, "Redemption means the reconciliation of God as well as the dominion of God. Therefore, Christ's priestly work is inseparable from His kingly role. Christ has abolished the figures of the law because he fulfills in His own person everything that the former priesthood typified. He is priest, victim, and altar."[127]

Christ's priestly office must be understood in the light of Old Testament prediction and New Testament fulfillment. Peterson says, "Yet, it is only in terms of its prediction of its Old Testament background that the uniqueness of Christ's priesthood stands out. In Christ, the

---

[125] Beeke, *Bible Doctrine*, 23.
[126] Ibid., 25.
[127] Cited in James Clarke, *Calvin's Doctrine of Work of Christ* (London: Camelot Press, 1956), 93.

priesthood and the ceremonies of the Old Covenant have come to their end."[128] This office is connected to atonement of the elect, the sanctified ones, who compose both the visible and invisible Church.

He is the High Priest because He undertook our infirmities; He became our real representative. By His gracious self-identification with our misery and hopelessness, He inspires us and gives us confidence in His redemptive work. The former priesthood could only typify atonement through animal sacrifice, but Christ is the real sacrifice, by which all our guilt is removed. He is the real Lamb of God whose blood takes away the sin of sinners. The former priests would come with an animal and shed its blood but Christ as the High Priest did not come to the altar with an animal but He Himself became the real sacrifice. He shed his blood to take away the sin of man (Heb. 9:11-13). When Christ came as high priest of the good things that are already here, He went through the greater and more perfect tabernacle that is not man-made, that is to say, not a part of this creation. He did not enter by means of the blood of goats and calves but He entered the Most Holy Place once for all by His own blood. Christ is the real altar. Christ's sacrifice needs no other ground than His own person. He is the atonement. He is the expiation and propitiation. God's wrath finds its deepest meaning and expression in the measureless sacrifice of His love.

Calvin asserts, "There is a connection between the two things, the sacrifice of the death of Christ, and his continual intercession (Rom. 8:34). These are the two parts of His priesthood; for, when Christ is called our priest, it is in this sense, that He once made atonement for our sins by His death so that He might reconcile us to God; that now having entered into the sanctuary of heaven, He appears in the presence of the Father in order to obtain grace for us, that we may be heard in His name."[129] Calvin says that Christ's intercession is the guarantee of our salvation and the basis of our confidence in our prayers. The prayer of Christ is a safe harbor, and whoever retreats into it is safe from danger of shipwreck. Calvin says that great benefits to the believers are Christ's ministry of intercession. Christians can enjoy peace of conscience knowing that God has fully accepted them in Christ, and that Christ

---

[128] Peterson, *Calvin and the Atonement*, 55.
[129] Ibid., 96.

continuously pleads their case before the Father. As Priest, Christ laid down His life for the elect, those who are redeemed by His blood. He shed His blood for the church.

John Owen writes, "By what means did Jesus Christ undertake the office of an external priest? By the decree, ordination, and will of God his Father, where He yielded voluntarily in obedience; so that concerning this there was a compact between them."[130] In the New Testament the book of Hebrews presents Christ as a sacrifice. B. B. Warfield says, "The biblical doctrine of the sacrifices of Christ finds full recognition in no other construction than that of the established church-doctrine of satisfaction. According to it, our Lord's redeeming work is at its core a true and perfect sacrifice offered to God, of intrinsic value ample for expiation of our guilt, and at the same time is true and perfect righteousness offered to God in fulfillment of the demand of His law."[131]

Christ's perfect sacrifice and satisfaction for sin produced the following wonderful results: He removed the guilt of sin and reconciled God with His people, He fully satisfied both God's justice and His love, enabling rejoicing in all God's attributes to be possible in the salvation of sinners. He secured a complete salvation for all saved sinners delivering from eternal death (hell), securing the right to eternal life (heaven), and restoring full communion with God. He produced a profound admiration and deep love in the hearts of all the saved.[132]

Christ is a priest and His praying work of intercession will continue until the end of the age. His prayers, as the perfect priest, will always be heard by the Father. Joel Beeke said in a lecture, April 29, 2008 in which he summarized three fundamental types of Christ' blessings which Christ bestows upon His people, the elect, "Temporal blessings relate to Christ's special care in His providence. He guards them with the apple of his eye (Deut. 32:10). He keeps and preserves the elect. Spiritual blessings include regeneration, converting and indwelling in

---

[130] John Owen, *The Glory of Christ*, Vol. 3 (Edinburgh: Banner of Truth Trust, 2000), 481.

[131] Benjamin Breckinridge Warfield, *The Person and Work of Christ* (Philadelphia: Presbyterian Reformed Publishing, 1950), 368.

[132] Beeke, *Bible Doctrine*, 27.

their hearts. He enlightens and inspires them. Eternal blessings relates to eternity, when they dwell with God forever in heaven."[133]

The Scriptures authenticate the priestly work of Christ. Christ's office of priesthood was planned by the Godhead before creation for the purpose of the redemption of the church.

CHRIST AS KING

The earthly kingdoms are based upon human organization, but Christ's kingdom is based upon power, grace, and glory. The kingly office is the third office of Christ. Christ rules as King, as God, as mediator and as ruler over the kingdom of glory. Brakel writes, "First as God, the Lord Jesus has within Himself all majesty, worthiness, honor, glory and power, even if there were no creatures. He is the King of the church. Other kings have but little power, are fully occupied in protecting themselves and their subjects, and are even conquered by others, but our King is 'the Almighty' (Rev. 1:8). Other kings die, are deposed, exiled, and cease to be kings. This King, however, 'shall be great, and shall be called the Son of the Highest: and the Lord God shall give unto Him the throne of His father David.'"[134] God has established Him in His kingdom and has consecrated Him by anointing (Psa. 2:6). As He did not exalt Himself to be a High Priest, He likewise did not exalt Himself to be King. That Christ was prophesied as the King in the Old Testament is evident from Psalm 2:6. Zechariah 9:9 confirms that. Richard Muller writes, "Christ's kingly office manifest manifests its power over the church as its head and his defense of the church against its enemies. Christ's office represents his post-resurrection work as well as the work of his earthly ministry, death, and resurrection: the threefold office demonstrates the unity of Christ's work."[135]

Christ's reign on earth and in heaven is the kingdom of power. It influences the physical world, governments, laws, institutions and civil society. In the kingdom of grace, His influence is of a spiritual nature,

---

[133] Joel R. Beeke, *"Christology,"* April 29, 2008.

[134] a' Brakel, *Christian's Reasonable Service*, vol. 1, 563.

[135] Richard A. Muller, *Christ and the Decree* (Grand Rapids: Baker, 1986), 141.

i.e., related to the souls of the people. Christ's church will reign with Him forever without sin, tears, pain, sorrow or death. There will be joy and celebration, worship, praises, singing, and glorifying of Him. Christ as King delivers His elect; He vindicates and preserves them. Christ as King governs and rules His elect righteously. Christ protects them from the attacks of evil and Satan and sin. Christ as the King of the universe, rules the earth. He enthrones and dethrones kings and rulers on earth (Dan. 2:21).

> If He had not, as our prophet, revealed the way of life and salvation to us, we could never have known it. Since we cannot know salvation apart from Him, it is also true that if He were not our High Priest and had not offered Himself up to obtain redemption for us, we could not have been redeemed by His blood. If we have been redeemed, still we need Him to live for us in the capacity of King, to apply this purchase of His blood to us so that we can have actual, personal benefit by His death. For what He revealed as a Prophet and purchased as a Priest, He applies as a King.[136]

Christ as King rules everything which is on earth and in heaven. He is the King of kings and Lord of lords. He rules over human beings, over both evil and good angels (Heb. 1:6), and over believers and unbelievers. He rules as the King of the church both in the Old Testament and New Testament. He will come to judge and to rule. His kingdom endures forever. The benefits of Christ's spiritual reign extend to the whole body of Christ's the church and to each believer. There are both temporary and eternal benefits for the believers. He will come to take His bride to be with Him for eternity. The church belongs to Christ, and He will redeem her forever. The office of kingship does not end. He will be the King of the church forever, for that was the purpose of redemption.

---

[136] Andrew Murray and John Flavel, *The Believer's Prophet, Priest and King* (Minneapolis: Bethany House, 1989), 63.

CONCLUSION

James Beeke says, "The work of Jesus Christ in His offices of Prophet, Priest, and King of His church is most rich and valuable. Christ's offices are connected to and interwoven with several other precious truths of Scripture. What a glorious Prophet, Priest, and King Jesus Christ is!"[137] Christ is presented as the Prophet, the High Priest, and the King by both the Old Testament and New Testament. The Old Testament confirmed His coming and His prophetic message and they were fulfilled in the New Testament as the High Priest and perfect sacrifice. The scriptures presented Him as King and Lord who will rule both the earth and heaven. He is the King of power, of grace and of glory. He rules evil and good angels, the elect and unbelievers. Satan is under His control because He holds the keys of Hades and He is the way, the truth, and the life (John 14:6).

Christ enthrones and dethrones kings according to His will. His Kingdom is for eternity with His elect, and the saints will dwell with Him in heaven forever. The three offices are both earthly and heavenly. Christ is the protector and defender of His church. He is the prophet for the church, the High Priest for the church, and the King of the church and of kings. He will return to take His church to Himself to live with Him eternally.

The sovereignty of the Godhead planned for the redemption of the elect long before the foundation of the world. Christ's three offices were designed for redemption and adoption of God's chosen people so that they would live with Christ forever.

---

[137] Beeke, *Bible Doctrine*, 45.

CHAPTER 5

THE CHURCH'S INCEPTION PRACTICALLY

The church of Jesus Christ is universal and in unity. Denominations are not the church, but they compose the universal church of Jesus Christ. He founded the church upon Himself and it belongs to Him and to Him alone. It is characterized by unity, universality, and perpetuity. All believers belong to one Lord and have the same Savior, one baptism, one faith, one Lord, one Spirit, and one destiny, hence they should love one another regardless of their differences in languages, race, and nationality.

The church on earth is a symbol of the invisible church in eternity. The church by its very essence and nature is the light and salt of the world. The universal church is united by the Lord's Supper as Christ initiated it and commanded that it should always be done in remembrance of Him as He orchestrated a New Covenant with His chosen people. His flesh is represented by the bread and His blood is represented by wine.

This chapter addresses the African church and the Zimbabwe church in particular as those churches are confronted on a daily basis with syncretism and other forms of church heresies. The chapter continues to reflect on the inception of the church before creation and shows that although the church is characterized by syncretism and acculturation, she is still part of the body of Christ.

THE UNIVERSAL CHURCH

John Calvin called the visible church "mother." Calvin asserts that, "But as it is now our purpose to discourse of the visible church, let us learn, from her single title of mother, how useful, now how necessary the knowledge of her is, since there is no other means of entering into her life unless she conceives us in the womb and give us birth, unless she nourish us at her breasts, and, in short, keep us under her charge and government until, divested of mortal flesh, we be like angels (Matt. 22:30)."[138] John Calvin wanted to portray that the church is the "Mother" who gives us birth and nourishes us with all the good food, i.e. good doctrines for our well-being. The universal church has some characteristics that are unique and are shared among the children of God. Calvin states,

> Hence the form of the Church appears and stands for conspicuous to our view. Wherever we see the Word of God sincerely preached and heard, wherever we see the sacraments administered according to the institution of Christ, there we cannot have any doubt that the church of God has some existence, since his promise cannot fail.... The universal church is the multitude collected out of all nations, who, though dispersed and far distant from each other, agree in one truth of divine doctrine, and are bound together by the tie of a common religion.[139]

This is a superb statement that summarizes the concept of the universal church. We the children of God are connected no matter where we are in the world. Christ as our Lord and Savior and the Bridegroom of the church ensures us that we are safe and that we do His will. The sacraments unite us as children of one family. As to the time that the universal church began, John Macquarrie comments, "The church is a necessary stage in this great action of being, so that to believe in

---

[138] Calvin, *Institutes,* 674.
[139] Ibid., 545.

creation is already to believe in the church and there is a sense in which the church was there in the beginning and is coeval with the world."[140]

The universal church unites all true believers in the world. The church is the large family of God where Christ unites His members through the work of the Holy Spirit. Those who are redeemed and are adopted into the family of God are initiated through the sacrament of water baptism.

The ordinance of baptism, though it was a Jewish practice, Christ accepted and confirmed it and commanded that it should be done (Matt. 28:19), which reflecting the unity of the Trinity. The Passover was also a Jewish practice, which was administered to the proselytes joining them from among the Gentiles. Christ adopted these two sacraments into the church. Baptism is an initiatory rite that incorporates the convert into the membership of the church. Anyone who believes and repents of his/her sins is baptized and becomes a member of the local church, and he/she partakes of the Lord's Supper with other members of the church as a sign of unity with Christ and with other members in the universal church. It is a spiritual truth embodied in an outward action. Bannerman states,

> The body washed with pure water was an emblem of the soul purified and cleansed through the blood and Spirit of Christ. The baptism for the remission of sin was expressive of the cleansing by which sin is removed. The action by which water was applied by the administrator to the person, was a representative of the application of the blood of Christ to the guilt of the soul. The action by which the washing of baptism was submitted to by the recipient, was expressive of the passing under the washing of regeneration and the renewing of the Holy Ghost.[141]

The second sacrament that Christ instituted in the church as a valuable ordinance was the Lord's Supper which He initiated as a new

---

[140] John Macquarrie, *Principles of Christian Theology* 2nd ed. (New York: Scribner's Publications, 1977), 311.

[141] Bannerman, *The Church of Christ*, 45.

covenant. The Lord's Supper marks the universality of the church and the unity among the believers. Bannerman states, "Christ, as head of the church, has dealt with a guarded hand merely of outward and visible rite which is baptism.... There is a second ordinance in a similar manner adapted for adults which is the Lord's Supper, accompanied by the preaching of the Gospel of Christ by sign as well as word, is a fleshly witness, speaking to the flesh as well as to the spirit of the believer, of the blessings of the covenant of grace."[142] These two sacraments are administered by a minister of the church. The gospel is the center of the two sacraments in the church of Christ. The contemporary church continues to administer the two sacraments as signs and marks of the true church. John Calvin defended the sanctity of the church and its sacraments as follows,

> How much the ministry of the word and sacraments should weigh with us, and how far reverence for it should extend, so as to be a perpetual badge for distinguishing the Church, has been explained; for we have shown, first, that whatever it exists entire and unimpaired, no error of conduct, no defects should prevent us from giving the name of Church; and, secondly, that trivial errors in this ministry ought not make us regard it as illegitimate.... "This is clearly evidenced by the words of Paul when he says, that the Church is, 'built upon the foundation of the apostles and prophets, Jesus Christ himself being the chief corner-stone" (Eph. 2:20). If the Church is the foundation of the apostles and prophets, by which believers are enjoined to place their salvation in Christ alone, then if that doctrine is destroyed, how can the Church continue to stand...? The communion of the Church was not instituted to be a chain to bind us to idolatry, impiety, ignorance of God, and other kinds of evil, but rather to retain us in the fear of God and obedience of the truth.[143]

---

[142] Ibid., 128.
[143] Ibid., 555.

The church exists in Christ alone. Actually in this quote, Calvin was refuting the Papacy which was distorting the sanctity of the church and perverting the governance of the church. According to Martin Luther's definition, a sacrament is that which is:

- Commanded by Christ;
- A promise of grace, and;
- Accompanied by an earthly element.

By this definition, only two commands concerning the sacraments by Christ fit this description: baptism and communion. In both cases the word of promise that is delivered is the forgiveness of sins. Of the seven sacraments instituted by the Catholic church, Luther rejected all but these two as true sacraments; the rest were either something not commanded by Christ (for instance, one does not *have* to get married, nor does one *have* to become ordained into the ministry in order to proclaim and profess Christianity) or they did not necessarily have the physical element attached (such as the Roman Catholic practice of confession). Admittedly, Luther was a bit more hesitant to throw confession aside as he did see confession and repentance as a command made by Christ to be practiced by every Christian. Thus in most Lutheran churches, both public and silent confessions of sin are made prior to the distribution of the sacrament of the Lord's Supper.[144]

Following Luther, the Reformers and the Protestant churches have also maintained only the two sacraments, Baptism and Lord's Supper. The sacraments unite the believers of ancient times to the present age. The church that originated before the creation of the world began to be realized shortly after the fall when people began to worship God corporately and grew when Israel became as a chosen nation. It was fully realized in the incarnation and fulfilled at Pentecost. It will continue for eternity when Christ comes for the second time to take His own to Himself at the end of the age.

Question 54 of the Heidelberg Catechism asks: "What do you

---

[144] Rebecca Craig, "Lutheran Sacrament: Understanding the use of Sacraments in the Lutheran Church," June 2, 2009, www.http://protestantism.suite101.com/article (Accessed February 13, 2010).

believe concerning 'the Holy Catholic Church'? I believe that, from the beginning to the end of the world, and from among the whole human race, the Son of God, by his Spirit and his Word, gathers, protests, and preserves for himself, in the unity of the true faith, a church chosen for eternal life. Moreover, I believe that I am and forever will remain a living member of it eternally."[145] Scholars disagree on what makes a church. Ramsay and Leith say, "The early Protestant taught that the church exists where the Word of God is rightly preached and taught and where the sacraments are rightly administered. According to them, the two distinguishing marks of the church are the preaching of the Word of God and the administration of the sacraments."[146] In the ancient words of the Apostle's Creed, the holy catholic Church is mentioned. The universality of the church means that it is composed of all races, all nationalities, all classes, all kinds of men and women and children. Cyril of Jerusalem contended:

> The Church, then, is called catholic because it is spread through the whole world, from one end of the earth to the other, and because it never stops teaching in all its fullness every doctrine that men ought to be brought to know: and that regarding things visible and invisible, in heaven and on earth. It is called a catholic church also because it brings into religious obedience every sort of men, ruler and ruled, learned and simple, and because it is a universal treatment and cure of every kind of sin whether perpetrated by soul and body, and possesses within it every form of virtue that is named, whether it expresses itself in deeds or words or in spiritual graces of every description.[147]

The concept of the universality of the church does not mean that it is the sum of many local churches added together but that each local

---

[145] William M. Ramsay and John H. Leith, *The Church, a Believing Fellowship* (Richmond: Covenant Life Curriculum Press, 1965), 89.

[146] Ibid., 90.

[147] Ibid., 93.

congregation is the catholic church. Catholicity is a quality which belongs to every congregation, as Cyril suggests. In Romans 10:11-12, Paul said, "For the scripture saith, whosoever believeth shall not be put to shame. For there is no difference between the Jew and the Greek: for the same Lord over all is rich unto all that call upon him." Christ is preparing His bride to present her before God the Father without blemish and wrinkle. Christ is gathering His church. He gathers His elect, the priesthood, and the family of God to Himself. Joel Beeke states, "Jesus gathers his church from all over the world by the Spirit of God, by preaching the Word of God. God comes to us in the darkness of our heart by the power of the Spirit and the power of His Word. Who gathers the church? The answer is Jesus gathers His church. How does He gather His church? He does it by His Word and Spirit. What does He gather? He gathers believers to Himself, the church, God's people, a peculiar people, and a holy nation."[148]

The unity of the church was envisioned by the apostle in Ephesians 4:3-4, "Making every effort to maintain the unity of the Spirit in the bond of peace. There is one body and one Spirit." Everett Ferguson propounds, "An important aspect of the church's witness to the larger society is displaying the unity that is essential to the church and is God's goal for humanity.... The unity of Christ with the Father is set forth as the image and goal of unity among believers.... Since Christ is one, the church must be one also. Christian unity derives from the cross of Christ."[149] The body of Christ exists in the world in unity and diversity. The unity and the catholicity of the church is grounded on Christ who owns the church from eternity. Wolfhart Pannenberg asserts,

> The unity of the church primarily involves concerns for the fellowship of the already existing churches with one another. Catholicity, by contrast, goes beyond the limits of the existing churches insofar as their present life still reveals elements of particularities and narrowness when seen in terms of their universal responsibility for mankind. The unity of the church is an internal issue,

---

[148] Joel Beeke, Sermon, "Christ Gathers His Church", recordings@hnrc.org, CD, 2009.

[149] Everett Ferguson, *The Church of Christ* (Grand Rapids: Eerdmans, 1996), 399.

both in reference to their unity with the origin and norm of the Christian community and the Christian faith. It involves the unity of the individual Christian with a specific community. The catholicity of the church goes beyond this to include the church's relationship to the world that is not yet permeated by the Christian faith.[150]

The living, invisible church is one despite diversity. The denomination that disregards the sacraments and the preaching of the Word, however, is not the church at all.

Avis quotes Hooper, "The attempt is therefore made by the English Reformers to identify the true church by its possession of the marks of the word and sacraments. These two marks, the true preaching of God's word and right use of the sacraments, declare what and where the true church is.... Where the doctrine is sound, and no idolatry defended, that church is of God, as far as mortal man can judge. And where this doctrine and right use of the sacraments be not, there is no church of Christ, though it seem never so holy (Ps. 2:8)."[151]

THE AFRICAN CHURCH

Missionaries have brought the Gospel to Africa. Some missionaries worked for their colonial powers while others engaged in evangelizing the people with the gospel. Those who aligned themselves with their colonial powers caused the Africans to shun the gospel because they were seen as part of the colonizers. In the early years of evangelization of Africa, church growth was very slow because of both colonization and mission work by the church. The Africans could not distinguish between the two institutions. When there were wars of liberation for independence, the Africans fought both institutions. Nevertheless, God used the missionaries to penetrate into all corners of Africa with the gospel. God used the missionaries to plant His church in the Africa

---

[150] Wolfhart Pannenberg, *The Church* (Philadelphia: Westminster Press, 1983), 61.

[151] Paul D. L. Avis, *The Church in the Theology of the Reformers* (London: Marshall Morgan & Scott Publications, 1981), 65.

which was regarded as a 'dark' continent, because there was little civilization measured by the standards of Western civilization. The continent was and still is regarded as third world because of the high level of poverty, underdevelopment, and illiteracy.

Spiritually, Africa is regarded as a religious continent due to its great variety of gods, idols, spirit mediums, and images. When the missionaries came and discovered that the indigenous people were worshipers of false gods, they introduced Christianity as an alternative religion. Latourette asserts, "Christianity entered as the hereditary faith of the Europeans.... The nineteenth century witnessed the penetration of this vast region by white explorers and merchants, and the partition of almost all territory among European powers."[152]

The first missionary to come to Zimbabwe was Robert Moffat in 1829. Robert Moffat concentrated on his role as a missionary, evangelist and teacher of the Christian faith. His greatest achievement was the translation of the Bible into the vernacular language of *IsiNdebele*, a *Zulu* dialect. John DeGruchy notes: "This concern through Bible translation to incarnate the gospel in the interior of southern Africa was made real in another way as well, enabling the local people to read the Bible in their own vernacular languages."[153]

After Moffat, David Livingstone soon arrived in South Africa and, subsequently, in Zimbabwe and then in Zambia and Malawi. He was a medical doctor, very different from the Africans. But, as DeGruchy writes: "Differences in color, speech, natural characteristics, religious belief, moral, social and intellectual condition, may stagger some about the unity of the race; but be it remembered that these diversities are mostly referable to external circumstances... The same pleasures, anxieties, crimes, virtues, vices, noble or mean actions and influences, affect alike in many instances the soul of the most cultivated philosopher and of the most uncivilized savage."[154] With the solid background of a missionary conception of an African world view which was shared abroad, so many

---

[152] Kenneth Scott Latourette, *The Great Century in the Americas: Australasia and Africa* (New York: Harper & Brothers, 1943), 319.

[153] John De Gruchy, *The London Missionary Society in Southern Africa, 1799-1999* (Athens: Ohio University Press, 2000), 27.

[154] Ibid., 37.

things happened thereafter. More missionaries came to Africa sent by missionary organizations. The partitioning of Africa in 1884-85, chaired by the German Chancellor, Bismarck, accelerated the colonization of Africa. The colonial governments brought in their cultures and traditions, and Christianity became part of the package for the Africans.

The genuine missionaries carried on evangelism, planting and building churches, and thus Christianity was introduced in Africa. There were some converts; they were taught the doctrines of the church, church polity, liturgies, hymns, Psalters, discipleship, discipline of the church, administration of the sacraments, and the preaching of the word of God. Although it was not done perfectly, Christ was building His church, visible, and invisible church in Africa. Today's need is great. As Wilbur O'Donovan writes:

> There is a great need in modern Africa for biblical Christianity.... The Church must be ready to offer solutions based in the Bible. The Church responds to the call to be the salt and light of the world in a corrupt and evil world (Matt. 5:13-14). There is much that is accepted as Christianity in Africa today that is not biblically Christianity. There are many churches that claim that they belong to the true church of Jesus and they are some who claim to be Christ or claim to lead true apostolic church. There are many people who call themselves prophets of God or apostles of Christ.[155]

The church in Africa is growing rapidly with churches swelling and sprouting in every corner. The reasons for that, according to some African scholars, is the shift of God's plan in fulfillment of the scriptures that Ethiopia will raise her hands to the Lord and she will be saved. Although there is massive church growth, it has been contended that there is a lack of depth of biblical knowledge, understanding, and teaching. This argument is debated among biblical scholars. O'Donovan notes: "One reason for the need for biblical Christianity in modern

---

[155] Wilbur O'Donovan, *Biblical Christianity in Modern Africa* (Carlisle: Paternoster Press, 2000), 217.

Africa is the presence of a large number of nominal Christians in the church."[156]

There is no visible church that is perfect on earth. Christ perfects His church through the renewal, regeneration, and transformation of believers by the work of the Holy Spirit who sanctifies them. There are many challenges in the African church. One of the major challenges is syncretism. Carson highlights that: "It is most significant that already at Jerusalem in 1928, at the second Meeting of the International Missionary Council, syncretism and secularization were being discussed as the problem of the church. In the light of resurgence of non-Christian religions, and increasing materialism and secularization in the West, the greatest enemies of Christian progress were seen to be, not other religions, but secularism and syncretism."[157] Basically, syncretism is strong in Africa and Asia, while the West is crippled by secularism.

The word syncretism was first used by Plutarch in a political sense to show a united front against a common enemy, *synkretismos.* "In the sixteenth century, the word was used to describe Bessarion's attempt to reconcile Plato and Aristotle. During the Reformation, the word retained its original political meaning in spite of profound differences, to combine forces against a common foe. Syncretism is defined as a systematic attempt to combine, blend and reconcile and inharmonious often conflicting religious elements."[158] Syncretism in Africa has assimilated into the church and has slowed down the genuine growth of believers. When people are converted, they usually continue in their old beliefs, especially in African Traditional Religion while they believe in in a new-found faith in Christ Jesus. Many of the believers continue to worship ancestor's spirits with their relatives and siblings in their villages while they have put their faith in Christ. They continue to wear strings of charms, with a belief that they will be protected by their long-dead relatives. They practice the traditional rituals; they carry ritual objects, and they consult the diviners, seers, the spirits of the dead, and the witch-doctors. They participate in traditional community rituals and believe in myths. Some who claim to be committed Christians

---

[156] Ibid., 218.
[157] Carson, *Church*, 259.
[158] Ibid., 263.

practice magic, sorcery, and witchcraft. This is an area that need to be examined and pray for complete surrender to Christ than to continue to hang on the old beliefs.

As the West is confronted with secularism, materialism, and humanism but Christ perfecting His church in the midst of all this secularism and materialism environment. Both words, syncretism and secularism, apply to Africa and Asia and the West. John Mite, an African theologian states, "All African peoples believe in God. They take this belief for granted. It is at the center of African religion and dominates all its other beliefs.... We know that it is a very ancient belief in African religious life."[159] While I agree that all African people believe in God, the question is, what kind of God do they believe? Do they believe in the Triune God, the God of the Bible, or another kind of god of their own perception? It is very true that the African people believe in God through His providential general revelation and special revelation in the new revelation through Christ and the Bible. However, before the special revelation, Africans believed in the god who was transcendent but not imminent, a God who does not have relationships with human beings but comes down to them to judge and punish, and to be served through sacrifices, gifts, appeasement, and worship. However, "God overlooked the times of ignorance but now demands all men everywhere to repent," (Acts 17:30).

As a minister in an African church in Zimbabwe, I have experienced that many believers were involved in syncretism. There is much need for counseling, teaching, and praying for the members of the church. Many of them are involved in spiritual warfare with the occult. One example of such practice happened to me in 1994, when one of the elders brought me a charm wrapped in a cloth with a large insect that he claimed was given by the witch-doctor for his protection twenty years before. That charm was so dirty that I could hardly tell that it was cloth. After hearing the message of Christ, he was convicted that day; he decided to surrender his charm to me to be burnt. I was terrified; I felt its heart beat in my hands. I later burnt it to ashes. This elder held the position of eldership for more than five years but, he was still not convicted that what he was practicing was wrong. They are many

---

[159] Mbiti, *African Religion*, 19.

examples like this which I have encountered as a minister in an African church. Some members are involved in witchcraft, sorcery, Satanism, and spiritual occult practices while being members of the church, having been baptized and participated in the Lord's Supper. This is the church the Lord Jesus died for to redeem her from her sins.

Other African scholars still contend that Jesus was or is the Messiah and Ancestor to the African peoples. Nyamiti writes: "The Shona and the Ndebele people believe in life in the here and now and talking of an eschatological Kingdom of God is actually meaningless to them; it is garbage. The interesting point to note here is the role of Jesus as healer, exorcist and preacher, in which activities he revealed his messiahship. In his capacity as a healer and exorcist, Jesus was a medicine man in his own culture (the so-called witchdoctor by Western sociologists). Jesus also practiced divination."[160]

This is one of the signs of the syncretistic stance. Some African theologians have the whole concept of the Bible and about Christ Jesus as their ancestor-messiah. Christ is God, Lord, Messiah, Savior, and Bridegroom of the universal invisible and visible church including the African church. The social gospel and a prosperity gospel is also affecting the African church. Bourdillon asserts:

> There are now many thousands of such churches spreading throughout Africa, ranging from small local sects, to large international churches with branches in perhaps half a dozen countries. There is also a wide range in style, from formal austere churches, differing little from the austere missionary churches in which the leaders of the new churches received their Christian training, to enthusiastic churches which emphasize healing and prophecy in long ritual punctuated by much singing. Independent churches began to emerge soon after the turn of the twentieth century, and were particularly numerous in South Africa.[161]

---

[160] Nyamiti, *Christ Our Ancestor*, 61.

[161] M. Bourdillon, *Religion and Society: A Text for Africa* (Gweru: Mambo Press, 1990), 271.

In the Independent churches are found syncretism, prophesying, exorcism, faith-healing, and the preaching of a social and a prosperity gospel. They misrepresent the church of Christ. It is critical to highlight that the Independent churches have distorted the true church of Jesus Christ because they mix the church with cultural, traditional, and customary beliefs and practices.

They are genuinely in error and their syncretism and secularism are not justifiable. They bring the world into the church instead of bringing the church into the world. They use the name of God in vain. The argument is not that the missionary churches were perfect and not prone to these defects, but as I have alluded in the previous chapters, the marks of the true church are the administering of the two sacraments believed and affirmed by the church of all ages. Christ still loves His church regardless of its state, but He warns us of the false prophets who will come in His name (Matt. 24:4-5).

Recent Christianity in Africa has brought distortions in the interpretation of the scriptures and the Church to some extent. Christianity is not a recent religion in Africa. If fact, it is very old in Africa. John Mbiti asserts,

> Christianity in Africa is so old that it can rightly be described as an indigenous, traditional, and African religion. Long before the start of Islam in the seventh century, Christianity was well established all over north Africa, Egypt, parts of the Sudan and Ethiopia. It was a dynamic form of Christianity, producing great scholars, and theologians like Tertullian, Origen, Clement of Alexandria, and Augustine. African Christianity made a great contribution to Christendom through scholarship, participation in Church councils, defense of faith, movements like monasticism, theology, translation, and preservation of the Scriptures, martyrdom, the famous Catechetical School of Alexandria, liturgy, and even heresies and controversies.[162]

---

[162] John S. Mbiti, *African Religions and Philosophy* (London: Heinemann Education, 1990), 223.

The African church has been characterized by Pentecostalism and a prosperity gospel, as well as the social gospel, as it sometimes called. Does it mean then that the African church is not part of the body of Christ? Far from it, in fact, the church is not perfect now but it is being made perfect by Christ through the work of the Holy Spirit, sanctifying her to the perfect image of Christ. One might argue that, because the church is not perfect now, do members have a license to abuse the church and to impose false doctrines, to manipulate people and abuse power in the name of the church of Jesus Christ? Of course, the Bible talks about the anti-Christ and false prophets who deceive many people in the world.

Christ spoke about the false prophets who would come and would deceive many people in His name (Matt. 24:4-10). In I John 4, John writes to his recipients that false prophets, false teachers, gnosticism, and the spirit of the anti-Christ would deceive many.

Syncretism is the problem of religious pluralism. There is a need for theological reconstruction:

> We should not focus on extracting principles from the Bible and applying these to culture. Scripture is not a book existing independent of us. Scripture is the living testimony to what God has done and continues to do, and we are part of that testimony....The application of Scripture is a gradual process of coming together, of life touching life. Our particular culture encounters the activity of God in building up a community of His people throughout history, a community that now includes us and our particular traditions, history and culture.[163]

Christianity is above cultures, it is stronger than every culture. The concept of the inception of the church before creation is a fundamental treasure indebted to the visible church. It serves as a reminder that no man can replace the church of Christ Jesus with a church his own

---

[163] Tokunboh, Adeyemo et al, *African Bible Commentary* (Nairobi: World Alive Publishers, 2006), 4.

institution and devised doctrines contrary to those of the true church. There is no excuse whatsoever to vindicate acculturation, secularism, humanism, and syncretism.

The true church of Jesus Christ remains the true church of Christ. Let the church be the church for all ages. The church, regardless where it located, should model Christ, the husband of the church. Christ is the prototype for the church. There is no excuse to plunge the church into syncretism, secularism, pluralism, or apostasies because of culture, tradition, or modernity prevailing in society. Cowan concludes with a fundamental truth in regards to the work of the Holy Spirit in convicting and converting sinners to Christ and bring to submission to Christ King of kings and Lords of lords: "Apart from the work of the Holy Spirit (Satan) will do all he can to resist the argument, even adopting extreme and outlandish beliefs rather than yielding the truth of Christian theism. But it is the role of the Holy Spirit to open the heart of the unbeliever and to use arguments as means of drawing people to himself."[164]

CONCLUSION

The universal church exists because of its nature, and her essence is bound to the bridegroom and the Head, Jesus Christ. John Calvin called the church "mother" because she gives birth to us and she nourishes the church. Regardless of the location the visible church is composed of many different people but they are united under Christ, the head of the church. The church is characterized by her catholicity, perpetuity, and unity. The two sacraments are administered in true church, Baptism, by immersion or sprinkling, and the Lord's Supper. The modern African church began through the work of missionaries in the 18th century, especially in Southern Africa. The church in recent years has been growing rapidly. However, independent churches have ushered in a new era of Christianity characterized by syncretism, and often promoting of a prosperity and social gospel. As a result, the true gospel has been twisted into a profit-oriented gospel. Christ is regarded as the traditional

---

[164] Gundary Cowan et al, *Five Views on Apologetics* (Grand Rapids: Zondervan, 2000), 53.

healer, exorcist, prophet, and witch-doctor *N'yanga* in *Shona* or *Inyanga* in *Ndebele/Zulu.*

Pentecostalism and syncretism is rife, promoting religious pluralism and the mixing of cultures and traditions with religion. However, there are many churches and denominations that are authentic and biblical, doctrinally sound and very faithful in maintaining the doctrines, confessions, and creeds of the ancient church in Africa. They are examples of the true church which is universal, perpetual, and united.

Theologians like Tertullian, Origen, Clement of Alexandria, and Augustine are the pride of the African church; they defended the faith and stood against all forms of heresies, distortions, syncretism, apostasies, and false prophets. They are the good examples of African theologians who understood their roles to preserve the heritage of the church. Christ continues to perfect His bride through the Holy Spirit's sanctifying everywhere in the world. The inception of the church stretches back to the Trinity before the foundation of the world. The invisible and universal members of the church were in Christ before creation.

CHAPTER 6

THE CHURCH'S INCEPTION SUMMARIZED

The inception of the church before creation with Christ as the head in His three-fold offices is a fundamental topic that ushers in an important paradigm of thinking in Christendom. It gives us a unique concept of the Trinity in the plan of the elect's salvation of the elect in the sovereign grace of God, showing His mercy, love, grace, and desire to save them. The church was realized in the Old Testament as YHWH chose Israel from among all the nations of the world as the type of the church that would be fulfilled in the New Testament with the incarnation of Christ. Christ sealed the existence of the church at the day of Pentecost when the Holy Spirit manifested Himself to the disciples in remarkable ways. This phenomenon confirmed the universality and the unity of the church.

The historical context of the church has been summarized as follows: The early church was represented by Simon Peter; the Patristic period was represented by Augustine of Hippo; the Medieval period was represented by Thomas Aquinas; the Reformation was represented by John Calvin; Post-Reformation was represented by John Bunyan and Evangelicalism was represented by George Whitefield. The concept of the inception of the church before creation is confirmed by Scripture in the doctrines of election, predestination, redemption and adoption. The visible and invisible church is ordained by God and is composed of the dead, the living, and the unborn. The visible church is characterized by catholicity, perpetuity, and unity in the two sacraments, baptism and the Lord's Supper.

The three offices of Christ as Prophet, Priest, and King serve as God; means to accomplish redemption of His elect, the chosen ones. The universal church is characterized by her universality, perpetuity, and unity. The African church is characterized by syncretism and acculturation while the western church is faced with secularism and materialism however the church still continues. Both in the West and in Africa, she has remained faithful even though she is challenged by secularism and syncretism, respectively.

When one contemplates how God created the world in six days by His spoken word and how all of creation responded to God's words until everything was in its proper place, it is a great wonder. The vegetation, all kinds of animals, insects, the living organisms in the oceans, the moon, the sun, the stars, and all the galaxies in the universe, display the power and the glory of God. At the time that He created Adam from the dust in His own image, all the elect, the chosen ones, were already predestined before the foundation of the world. Have you ever contemplated that?

Everything about election, predestination and redemption was already preplanned. The counsel of the Godhead is foreknown to God, so that the church was already conceived in God's mind from eternity. This is mystery beyond human understanding. It is wonderful and so consoling to know that all the children of God whether dead or alive or unborn, were already in the plan of the Godhead, chosen already before the foundation of the world. It was in God's will and pleasure to choose us and determine to sacrifice His Son before we were born. He chose us before we were in our mother's womb. "Before I formed you in the womb I knew you; before you were born I sanctified you; and I ordained you a prophet to the nations" (Jer. 1:5). What did He choose if we were not born? Truly, the physical, the material and the visible reflect the invisible in a mysterious way. It is an indicative phenomenon of God's grace, mercy, and love that should us to ponder the depth of God's love every second of our lives. What an amazing God we have – a God who can decree to love, forgive, redeem, and adopt us before we were born!

This theme is fundamentally important for the life of every believer who thinks about his/her past, present, and future in the hands of the merciful God. Election before the foundation of the world is a special act of God toward a sinner and adopting him/her to be in the family of God. I pray that this thesis will be a meaningful and useful document for the church, for seminaries, and for universities as a heritage of the church. It traces the plan of the Godhead, to the Old Testament when the church was realized in the children of Israel; to the New Testament when it was fulfilled in the incarnation of the God-man, Christ Jesus, on the day of Pentecost, as the Holy Spirit sealed the church; and to all in eternity when Christ fetches His bride, the church, to be with Him forever.

Christ was the Prophet of prophets in the Old Testament instructing, giving messages, and informing the prophets to tell the Israelites that the Messiah would come to deliver them from their bondage and sins. As the Priest of priests, He not only brought the sacrifice, but He became the altar and sacrifice. He became the atonement for the church to redeem her. As the King of kings and Lord of lords, He will reign with power and glory with His elect over the universal church.

BIBLIOGRAPHY

a' Brakel, William. *The Christian's Reasonable Service*. vol. 1. Ligonier: Soli Deo Gloria, 1992.

Adeyemo, Tokunboh et al. *African Bible Commentary*. Nairobi: World Alive, 2006.

Avis, Paul D. L., *The Church in the Theology of the Reformers*. London: Marshall Morgan & Scott, 1981.

Baker, Charles F. *Bible Truth-What We Believe and Why We Believe it*. Milwaukee: Milwaukee Bible College, 1956.

Bannerman, Douglas D. *The Scripture Doctrine of the Church*. Grand Rapids: Eerdmans Publishers, 1955.

Bannerman, James. *The Church of Christ*, vol.2. London: The Banner of Truth Trust, 1960.

Beeke, James W. *Bible Doctrine for Teens and Young Adults*. Grand Rapids: WM. B. Eerdmans, 1988.

Beeke, Joel. *Calvin for the 21ˢᵗ Puritan Reformed Conference*: August 27-29 Grand Rapids: Calvin College Prince Conference Center, 2009.

_____. *Christology*. Lecture, April 29, 2008.

_____. *Christology*. Lecture 13, March 19, 2008.

_____. Sermon, "Christ Gathers His Church." Grand Rapids: recordings@hnrc. org, DC October 4, 2009. (Accessed March 20, 2010).

_____. *"The Soul of Life": The Piety of John Calvin*. Grand Rapids: Reformation Heritage Books, 2009.

_____. Sermon, '*Ten Happy Truths About Election*,' Grand Rapids: recording@ hnre.org, October 11, 2009, CD (Accessed March 16, 2010).

Belden, Albert D. *George Whitefield. The Awaken*. London: Rock cliff, 1953.

Beza, Theodore. *The Life of John Calvin*. New York: Evangelical Press, 1997.

Bickersteth, Edward H. *The Trinity.* Grand Rapids: Kregel, 1976.

Bourdillon, M. *Religion and Society: A Text for Africa.* Gweru: Mambo Press, 1990.

Breckinridge, Benjanmin W. *The Person and Work of Christ.* Philadelphia: The Presbyterian Reformed, 1950.

Calvin, John. *John Calvin Institutes of the Christian Religion.* Translated by Henry Beveridge. Peabody: Hendrickson, 2008.

Calvin, John. *Calvin's Institutes.* Grand Rapids: Associated Publishers, 1564.

_____. *Commentaries on the Epistles of Paul to the Galatians and Ephesians.* Grand Rapids: Baker Book House, 1996.

_____. *Institutes of the Christian Religion.* Philadelphia: Westminster Press, 1960.

_____. *Sermons on the Epistle to the Ephesians.* Edinburgh: Banner of Truth Trust, 1973.

Carson, D. A. *The Church in the Bible and the World.* Grand Rapids: Baker Book House, 1987.

Clark, Gordon H. *Predestination.* New Jersey: Presbyterian and Reformed, 1969.

Clarke, James. *Calvin's Doctrine of Work of Christ.* London: Camelot Press, 1956.

Clearwaters, Richard V. *The Local Church of the New Testament.* Chicago: Conservative Baptist Association, 1954.

Collmer, Robert G. *Bunyan in our Time.* Kent: State University Press, 1989.

Colyar, Nelson R. *Expository Notes on the Book of Ephesians.* Little Rock: The Challenge Press, 1972.

Copleston, F. C. *Aquinas.* Baltimore: Penguin, 1965.

Custance, Arthur C. The *Virgin Birth and the Incarnation.* Grand Rapids: Zondervan, 1980.

Dallimore, Arnold A. *George Whitefield,* vol. 1. Edinburgh: Banner of Truth Trust, 1989.

David, Garner. "Adoption in Christ." Ph.D. dissertation, Westminster Theological Seminar, 2002.

Davidson, Ivor J. *The Birth of the Church,* vol. 1. Grand Rapids: Baker, 2004.

Davies, Brian. *The Thought of Thomas Aquinas.* Oxford: Clarendon Press, 1993.

De Gruchy, John . *The London Missionary Society in Southern Africa: 1799-1999.* Athens: Ohio University Press, 2000.

Dix, Kenneth. *John Bunyan, Puritan Pastor.* Northamptonshire: The Fauconberg Press, 1978.

Douglas, J. D. *The New Bible Dictionary.* Grand Rapids: Eerdmans, 1962.

Dowley, Tim. *Introduction to the History of Christianity.* Minneapolis: Fortress Press, 2002.

Dyer, Thomas H. *The Life of John Calvin.* New York: Harper, 1850.

Eaton Michael, A. *Focus on Hosea. Ross-shine*, U.K.: Christian Focus, 1996.

Edersheim, Alfred. *The Life and Times of Jesus the Messiah.* Grand Rapids: Eerdmans, 1981.

Edgar, Brian. *The Message of the Trinity.* Downers Grove, Il: InterVarsity Press, 2004.

Estelle, Bryan D., Fesko, J. V., and Adeyemo, Tokunboh. *African Bible Commentary.* Nairobi: World Alive, 2006.

Farthering, John L. *Thomas Aquinas and Gabriel Biel.* London: Duke University Press, 1988.

Ferguson, Everett. *The Church of Christ.* Grand Rapids: Eerdmans, 1996.

Filbeck, David. *Yes, God of the Gentiles, Too: The Missionary Message of the Old Testament.* Wheaton: Billy Graham Centre, 1994.

Frederick, John J. *Calvin's Doctrine of the Work of Christ.* London: James Clark, 1956.

Freedman, David N. *Eerdmans Dictionary of the Bible.* Grand Rapids: Eerdmans, 2000.

Furlong, Monica. *Puritan's Progress.* New York: Coward, McConn and Geoghegan, 1975.

Gadsby, John. *Slavery, Adoption and Redemption.* New Ipswich: Pietan, 1994.

Gaebelein, Frank E. and Douglas, J. *The expository Bible Commentary.* vol. 2. Grand Rapids: Zondervan, 1978.

MacGreg, Geddes. *Corpus Christi.* Philadelphia: The Westminster Press, 1958.

George, Johnston. *The Doctrine of the Church in the New Testament.* Cambridge: University Publications, 1943.

George, Timothy. *God the Holy Trinity.* Grand Rapids: Baker Academic, 2006.

Goldingay, John. *Old Testament Theology.* vol. 1. Downers Grove: Intervarsity Press, 2003.

Grabowski, Stanislaus J. *The Church: An Introduction to the Theology of St. Augustine.* St. Louis: B. Herder, 1957.

Gray, C. James, and George M. Adams. *Gray & Adams' Bible Commentary*. Grand Rapids: Zondervan, 1903.

Greaves, Richard L. *John Bunyan*. Grand Rapids: Eerdmans, 1969.

Grisworld, Ferrell. *Particular Redemption*. Florida: Chapel Library, (n. d.).

Gundary, Cowan. et al, *Five Views on Apologetics*. Grand Rapids: Zondervan, 2000.

Guralnik, David B. *Webster's New World Dictionary*. New York: World Publishing Company, 1970.

Hanke, Howard A. *From Eden to Eternity*. Grand Rapids: Eerdmans, 1960.

Henry, Matthew. *Matthew Henry Commentary*. Virginia: Macdonald, n. d.

Hiebert, Edmond D. *1 Peter*. Chicago: Moody Press, 1992.

Hyma, Albert. *The Life of John Calvin*. Grands Rapids: B. Eerdmands, 1943.

Ironside, H. A. *In the Heavenly: Practical Expository Address on the Epistle to the Ephesians*. Neptune, New Jersey: Loizeaux Brothers, 1979.

Israel, Gerard, and Lebar, Jacques. *When Jerusalem Burned*. New York: William Morrow & Company, 1973.

Johnston, E. A. *George Whitefield: A Definitive Biography*. vol. 1. London: Tentmaker, 2008.

Latourette, Kenneth S. *The Great Century in the Americas, Australasia, and Africa*. New York: Harper & Brothers, 1943.

Letham, Robert. *The Holy Trinity*. Phillipsburg: P & R, 2004.

Lillie, John. *Lectures on the First and Second Epistles of Peter*. Minnesota: Klock and Klock, 1978.

Lincoln, Andrew. *Word Biblical Commentary: Ephesians*. Nashville: Thomas Nelson, 1990.

Macquarrie, John. *Principles of Christian Theology*. Second ed. New York: Scribner's Publications, 1977.

Mastertown, Charles. *The Doctrine of the Holy Trinity*. Edinburgh: Andrew Elliot, 1880.

Mbiti, John S. *African Religions and Philosophy*. London: Heinemann Education Publications, 1990.

_____. *African Religions and Philosophy*. London: Heinemann Education, 1990.

_____. *Introduction to African Religion*. London: Heinemann International Literature, 1975.

McMahon, Matthew C. *A Puritan Mind*. Website Maven, 2009.

Meeter, Henry. *The Life of John Calvin*. Grand Rapids: Calvin College Bookstore, 1947.

Metzger, Bruce M. *The Eerdmans Bible Dictionary*. Grand Rapids: WM. B. Eerdmans, 1987.

Micklem, Nathaniel. *The Doctrine of our Redemption*. Nashville: Abingdon-Cokesbury Press, 1948.

Montgomery, James B. *Romans*. Grand Rapids: Baker, 1993.

Motyer, Alec. *Look to the Rock: an Old Testament Background to our Understanding of Christ*. Grand Rapids: Kregel, 2004.

Muller, Richard A. *Christ and the Decree*. Grand Rapids, Michigan: Baker, 1986.

Murray, Andrew, and Flavel, John. *The Believer's Prophet, Priest and King*. *Minneapolis:* Bethany, 1989.

Murray, John. *Redemption Accomplished and Applied*. Grand Rapids: Eerdmans, 1955.

Murrell, Standford E. *A Glorious Institution: The Church in History*. Pensacola: Mount Zion, 1998.

Myers, Allen C. *The Eerdman Bible Dictionary*. Grand Rapids: William B. Eerdmans, 1987.

Nyamiti, C. *Christ Our Answer: Christology from an African Perspective*. Gweru: Mambo Press, 1984.

O'Donovan, Wilbur. *Biblical Christianity in Modern Africa*. Cumbria: Paternoster Press, 2000.

Owen, John. *Biblical Theology*. Morgan, PA: Soli Deo Gloria, 1994.

_____. *The Glory of Christ., vol.3 of Works* Edinburgh: The Banner of Truth Trust, 2000.

Pannenberg, Wolfhart. *The Church*. Philadelphia: Westminster Press, 1983.

Peterson, Robert A. *Calvin and the Atonement*. Ross-Shire: Christian Focus, 1999.

_____. *Adopted by God*. Phillipsburg: P & R, 2001.

Philpot, J. C. *Meditations on the First Chapter of the Epistle to the Ephesians*. Harperden: Gospel Standard Strict Baptist Trust, 1978.

Polman, A. D. R. *The Word of God According to St. Augustine*. Grand Rapids: Eerdmans, 1961.

Radmacher, Earl D. *What the Church is All About*. Chicago: Moody Press, 1972.

Ramsay, William M. and John H. Leith. *The Church a Believing Fellowship*. Richmond, Virginia: The Covenant Life Curriculum Press, 1965.

Rebecca, Craig. Lutheran Sacrament: Understanding the use of Sacraments in the Lutheran Church. June 2, 2009, www.http://protestantism.suite101.com/article (Accessed February 14, 2010).

Renick, Timothy M. *Aquinas for Armchair Theologians.* Louisville: Westminster John Knox Press, 2002.

Seock-Tae, Sohn. *The Divine Election of Israel.* Grand Rapids: William B. Eerdmans, 1991.

_____. *YHWH, the Husband of Israel.* Oregon: Wipf and Stock, 2002.

Sharrock, Roger. *John Bunyan.* New York: St. Martin's Press, 1968.

Spence, H. D. M. and Joseph S. Exell. *The Pulpit Commentary.* Grand Rapids: Eerdmans, 1962.

Sproul, R. C. *The Purpose of God: Ephesians.* Ross-Shire: Christian Focus, 2006.

Spurgeon, Charles H. *Christ's Incarnation.* Pasadena: Pilgrim Publications, 1978.

Stevenson-Moessner, Jeanne. *The Spirit of Adoption.* Louisville: Westminster John Knox Press, 2003.

Thompson, Colin. *Revival, Newsline:"The Reformation and Revival Fellowship."* Spring 2005, 569.

Tokunboh, Adeyemo. *African Bible Commentar.* Nairobi: World Alive, 2006.

Toon, Peter. and Spiceland, James D. *One God in Trinity.* London: Samuel Bagster, 1980.

Unger, Merrill F. *The New Unger's Bible Dictionary.* Chicago: Moody Press, 1988.

Valentine, S. R. *John Bennet & the Origins of Methodism and the Evangelical revival in England.* Lanham: Scarecrow Press, 1997.

Vanderwaal, Cornelius. *Search the Scripture,* vol. 9. Ontario: Paideia Press, 1979.

Van Drunen David. *The Law is Not Faith.* Phillipsburg: P & R, 2009.

Verbraken, Patrick. *The Beginnings of the Church.* New York: Paulist Press, 1968.

Ware, Bruce A. *Father, Son, and Holy Spirit.* Wheaton: Good News Publishers, 2005.

Wilberforce, Robert I. *The Doctrine of the Incarnation of Our Lord Jesus Christ in its Relationship to Mankind and to the Church.* Philadelphia: H. Hooker, 1849.

Printed in the United States
By Bookmasters